# BRASSED OFF

by Paul Allen

Adapted from the screenplay
by Mark Herman

Copyright © 2005, 2022 by Paul Allen and Mark Herman
All Rights Reserved

*BRASSED OFF* is fully protected under the copyright laws of the British Commonwealth, including Canada, the United States of America, and all other countries of the Copyright Union. All rights, including professional and amateur stage productions, recitation, lecturing, public reading, motion picture, radio broadcasting, television, online/digital production, and the rights of translation into foreign languages are strictly reserved.

ISBN 978-0-573-01996-8

concordtheatricals.co.uk
concordtheatricals.com

## FOR AMATEUR PRODUCTION ENQUIRIES

UNITED KINGDOM AND WORLD
EXCLUDING NORTH AMERICA
licensing@concordtheatricals.co.uk
020-7054-7298

Each title is subject to availability from Concord Theatricals,
depending upon country of performance.

CAUTION: Professional and amateur producers are hereby warned that *BRASSED OFF* is subject to a licensing fee. The purchase, renting, lending or use of this book does not constitute a licence to perform this title(s), which licence must be obtained from the appropriate agent prior to any performance. Performance of this title(s) without a licence is a violation of copyright law and may subject the producer and/or presenter of such performances to penalties. Both amateurs and professionals considering a production are strongly advised to apply to the appropriate agent before starting rehearsals, advertising, or booking a theatre. A licensing fee must be paid whether the title is presented for charity or gain and whether or not admission is charged.

This work is published by Samuel French, an imprint of Concord Theatricals Ltd.

The Professional Rights in this play are controlled by United Agents LLP, 12-26 Lexington St, London W1F 0LE

No one shall make any changes in this title for the purpose of production. No part of this book may be reproduced, stored in a retrieval system, scanned, uploaded, or transmitted in any form, by any means, now known or yet to be invented, including mechanical, electronic, digital, photocopying, recording, videotaping, or otherwise, without the prior written permission of the publisher. No one shall share this title, or part of this title, to any social media or file hosting websites.

The moral right of Paul Allen and Mark Herman to be identified as author of this work has been asserted in accordance with Section 77 of the Copyright, Designs and Patents Act 1988.

## USE OF COPYRIGHTED MUSIC

A licence issued by Concord Theatricals to perform this play does not include permission to use the incidental music specified in this publication. In the United Kingdom: Where the place of performance is already licensed by the PERFORMING RIGHT SOCIETY (PRS) a return of the music used must be made to them. If the place of performance is not so licensed then application should be made to PRS for Music (www.prsformusic.com). A separate and additional licence from PHONOGRAPHIC PERFORMANCE LTD (www.ppluk.com) may be needed whenever commercial recordings are used. Outside the United Kingdom: Please contact the appropriate music licensing authority in your territory for the rights to any incidental music.

## USE OF COPYRIGHTED THIRD-PARTY MATERIALS

Licensees are solely responsible for obtaining formal written permission from copyright owners to use copyrighted third-party materials (e.g., artworks, logos) in the performance of this play and are strongly cautioned to do so. If no such permission is obtained by the licensee, then the licensee must use only original materials that the licensee owns and controls. Licensees are solely responsible and liable for clearances of all third-party copyrighted materials, and shall indemnify the copyright owners of the play(s) and their licensing agent, Concord Theatricals Ltd., against any costs, expenses, losses and liabilities arising from the use of such copyrighted third-party materials by licensees.

## IMPORTANT BILLING AND CREDIT REQUIREMENTS

If you have obtained performance rights to this title, please refer to your licensing agreement for important billing and credit requirements.

# BRASSED OFF

First performed at the Crucible Theatre, Sheffield, on 17th March, 1998, with the following cast:

| | |
|---|---|
| GLORIA | Freya Copeland |
| DANNY | Peter Armitage |
| SANDRA | Kate McGeever |
| ANDY | James Thornton |
| PHIL | Shaun Dooley |
| RITA | Rita May |
| VERA | Shaaron Jackson |
| HARRY | Bill Rogers |
| JIM | Stephen Bent |
| SHANE | Luke Pearce/Andrew Smith |
| CRAIG | Luke Strutt/Tom Damms |
| MELODY | Kerry Whittaker/Carla Pickering |

Music performed by Grimethorpe Colliery Band

The play was directed by Deborah Paige
Decor by Roger Glossop and Pip Leckerby
Lighting by Richard Owen

## AUTHOR'S NOTE

## NOTES ON STAGING

The play takes place in Shane's memory. He was eight when the action took place but he is recalling it with hindsight. The age of the actor who plays Shane, therefore, is determined by a decision as to when the play is being staged. Realistically he would be 19 in 2005, but the play was first performed successfully with 12-year-olds and it is useful to suggest that he is still a child.

As indicated in the script, the parts of the hospital nurses can be doubled. It is also easy to reduce them to a single nurse if desired. The bailiffs can be doubled by the actors playing Jim and Harry. The trophy at the Albert Hall can be brought on by stage management but ideally it would be a middle-aged man in a suit.

It is set in a number of different locations—homes in a mining village, the pithead, picturesque parts of Lancashire, a hospital and the Albert Hall among them. The staging needs to be flexible rather than detailed. A permanent suggestion of the pithead winding gear seems essential, but other locations should be indicated as economically and speedily as possible and it has been successfully produced on a stage that is almost completely bare. Although the play is divided into scenes for convenience, the action is continuous and overlapping; where possible actors should be in the appropriate location before the previous scene ends, and the start of the following scene can, if necessary, be indicated by a lighting change.

Ideally the band should be seen only when on stage: at the very start, in the first rehearsal scene, marching at Saddleworth, at the start of Act II, appearing as a small group at the hospital, and performing at the Albert Hall. However, bands which are less mobile or theatres with small stages may make it necessary to station bands permanently in one place which can be included in the action when appropriate but left in darkness at other times.

It is possible, especially in a proscenium arch theatre, for Gloria to mime while somebody else plays the flugelhorn in the *Nessun Dorma* audition. But there is a particular thrill if she can really play.

# BRASSED OFF

Subsequently presented by Sheffield Theatres by arrangement with Channel 4, Miramax Films and Prominent Features at the Olivier Theatre, Royal National Theatre, on 8th June 1998, with the following cast:

| | |
|---|---:|
| GLORIA | Freya Copeland |
| DANNY | Peter Armitage |
| SANDRA | Kate McGeever |
| ANDY | Adrian Bower |
| PHIL | Shaun Dooley |
| RITA | Rita May |
| VERA | Shaaron Jackson |
| HARRY | Bill Rogers |
| JIM | Stephen Bent |
| SHANE | Luke Pearce/Andrew Smith |
| CRAIG | Edward Savage |
| MELODY | Lauren Bird |

Other parts were played by Douglas Henderson, George Janopulos and Goran Kostic

Music performed by members of Avery and Newham Band and Redbridge Brass

The play was directed by Deborah Paige
Decor by Roger Glossop and Pip Leckerby
Lighting by Richard Owen

## CHARACTERS

DANNY, ex-miner, veteran conductor of Grimley Band
PHIL, his son, miner and trombone player, about 35
SANDRA, Phil's wife
JIM, somewhat older miner and euphonium player
VERA, Jim's wife
HARRY, Jim's inseparable companion in pit and band: a big E flat bass player (tuba)
RITA, Harry's wife
ANDY, a miner and tenor horr. player, about 25
GLORIA, newly returned to Grimley, an excellent flugelhorn player, about 25
SHANE, son of Phil and Sandra, aged 8 in 1994, but now older (see notes on staging)
CRAIG and MELODY, Shane's younger brother and sister

BAILIFFS, NURSES, MINERS, etc., played by members of the company

### BRASS BAND PLAYERS

The action takes place in various locations–prominent among them a mining community in the north of England, the pithead, parts of Lancashire, a hospital and the Royal Albert Hall, London.

Time: 1994 and following.

# ACT I

### Scene One

*Overture: **"DEATH OR GLORY"**; the music starts in darkness, played by the band on stage.*

*The lamps of pit helmets emerge from the encompassing gloom, worn by the cast and maybe on-stage band members.*

*During the introductory music the stage lights come up and then we hear a pit cage clang shut. Helmets are removed and lights switched off.*

*The band exits as* **SHANE** *comes downstage, leaving the rest of the cast grouped us:* **JIM**, **HARRY**, **PHIL** *and* **ANDY** *at the front, the* **WOMEN** *(except* **GLORIA**) *behind with* **CRAIG** *and* **MELODY**, *and* **GLORIA**, *wearing a smart business suit, and* **DANNY** *at the very back, perhaps with his bike.* **SHANE** *holds a presentation baton and* **DANNY**'s *band uniform jacket. He switches freely from addressing the audience to engaging with the rest of the cast throughout.*

**SHANE**  This happened in nineteen ninety-four. I were only eight. I weren't even born in pit strike, but you're supposed to know about it, born or not. Me dad were an 'ero, I know that.

> **PHIL** *leads other miners–***JIM**, **HARRY**, **ANDY**–*as they make to go to work.*

PHIL  I don't want to hear you've been in trouble, Shane, all right? Give yer mam a hand.

SHANE  Me dad and his mates, uncle Jim and uncle Harry, what live up our road.

JIM  Shane, lad.

HARRY  All right, Shane.

SHANE  And Andy...

ANDY  Ey, up, lads.

SHANE  ...he's the one following on.

*The men go.*

*VERA and RITA peel off towards SHANE while SANDRA and the kids take over the "house" space. VERA has a few sweets in a bag.*

VERA  Here y'are, Shane. Two for you. two for Craig and two for Melody. You will give 'em to 'em, won't you?

SHANE  Course I will, Auntie Vera.

VERA  Good lad. *(To RITA, as they go)* He is a good boy.

RITA  Ay, considering. Shame they have to grow up.

*RITA and VERA exit.*

SHANE  Me auntie Vera who works in supermarket. Two sweets each. I'll give Craig and Melody one each, 'cos they're always fighting. Then there's four for me. Could give me mam one. Not Kylie though. She's only a babby.

SANDRA  You scuff them trainers, Shane Ormondroyd and you'll feel the back of my hand!

SHANE  Me mam's mental. It's 'cos we've got no money, I think.

*Only DANNY is left of the original group as GLORIA approaches SHANE.*

**GLORIA**  D'you know where the Lantern Hotel is?

**SHANE**  Ay, I do, thanks. *(Very annoying: he enjoys it)* Up road, on left.

**GLORIA**  Thanks.

**SHANE**  Watch your car for a quid, Miss?

**GLORIA**  I'll tell your mother about you.

**SHANE**  She'll want a fiver.

> *But* **GLORIA** *is gone.*
>
> She in't from round here. Even men don't wear suits round here.

**DANNY**  Shane, lad.

**SHANE**  Me grandad! He's me dad's dad. *(He hands* **DANNY** *the jacket and the baton)*

**DANNY**  Make sure your dad's not late for band practise, will you, Shane?

**SHANE**  Yes, Grandad.

> **DANNY** *goes.*
>
> It's two o'clock. Me dad's on earlies, so he's just coming off shift. That gives him…six hours till practise. He will be late though.

**SANDRA**  Shane!

**SHANE**  Grimley. Near Barasley. Yorkshire. England. The world. The universe. This is our house. Just up from video, off-licence and nearly-new shop…

**SANDRA**  Shane!

> *Instead of kicking anything,* **SHANE** *mimes heading a golden goal before going "indoors" just as* **PHIL** *does the same in the locker room.*

**SHANE**  Yessss! Ormondroyd!

## Scene Two

> **PHIL**, *in the locker room, is just dressed after a shower. He mimes simultaneously and identically to* **SHANE**, *and then takes the applause of the crowd.*

**PHIL** Yesss! Ormondroyd...

> **HARRY**, *close behind, clocks* **PHIL**'s *goal but concentrates on the perfection of his ageing rocker's haircut.*

**HARRY** You straight home, Phil, or coming for a wet?

**PHIL** *(patting his pockets but knows he's skint)* Straight home, Harry.

**HARRY** I'm in the chair.

**PHIL** No, it's not that. Stuff to do, tha knows...

**HARRY** What did you have for snap today?

**PHIL** Oh...the usual.

> **JIM** *appears, studying a sheet of paper—a union memo.*

**JIM** We're stuffed, lads.

**PHIL** What's up, Jim?

**JIM** Barmston's voted to take the money. Four to one in favour of closure. Twelve hundred jobs gone! As of now.

**PHIL** Bloody Barmston! Ay, well, Barmston. They were never that solid.

**JIM** They were *rock* solid in eighty-four. Just cos they never had a pitched battle with bobbies, Phil. They were solid as us. Going for a wet, Harry?

**HARRY** Twist me arm, I might.

**PHIL** Grimley won't vote for money though, will we?

**JIM** Twenty thousand quid a man, Phil? What do you think?

PHIL  Not ours to sell though, is it? You're selling the jobs of them that come after. You said that.

HARRY  You really want your Craig and Shane to spend their lives down this lot?

PHIL  They should have choice. Bugger all else, Harry. Barmston'll be dead this time next year. Shops all shuttered up, blokes at home watching Richard and Judy. If they can keep up payments on telly. Women doing part-time jobs in supermarket.

JIM  My missus does that.

PHIL  Ay, for a bit extra, not to feed family. Any road, supermarket'll probably close down. Right, lads. Catch you at band.

JIM  See you, Phil. *(He watches as* PHIL *goes)*

PHIL *exits.*

Is he all right?

HARRY  Won't say owt, Jim.

ANDY, *always last and not quite dressed, arrives in time to hear the following.*

I tried to get him to come down the boozer, my shout, but he wouldn't have it.

ANDY  Your shout, Harry?

JIM  Oh, here he comes, Fast bloody Eddie. Andy, lots of us drag us heels a bit when we're going on shift but you're the only one I know who's slow going off an' all.

ANDY  He's not ready yet. *(He means* HARRY*)*

HARRY  I am.

ANDY  You're not.

HARRY  I am.

*ANDY ruffles HARRY's carefully constructed quiff and gets a hand covered in grease for his pains.*

**ANDY** Yurgh!

**JIM** I can remember when he'd've decked you for that.

**HARRY** It's not too late. *(But he's putting his hair back together)*

**JIM** Bloody Barmston. We can win this if we make sure it goes to review.

**ANDY** Make sure what goes to review?

**JIM** Ballot next week! Where've you bin?

**HARRY** He's winding you up, Jim.

**ANDY** Aren't you lot ready yet? I'm due on snooker table.

**HARRY** I pity some poor lass.

**ANDY** Why?

**HARRY** You're gonna have to settle down some day and she's gonna have to take you in hand.

**JIM** No, he gets enough of that already. That's the trouble. Not like our day, Harry. Decent lasses wanted commitment before legover.

**ANDY** I worry about you old guys. You don't think about nowt 'cept sex. Come on. I'll fix you up with some lasses.

*As the men make to leave, they cross with RITA at the head of a small group of "Women Against Pit Closures"– who chant in unison.*

**WOMEN** The miners, united, will never be defeated.

The miners, united, will never be defeated.

**RITA** Say no to bloody blackmail. Say yes to miners' jobs.

**HARRY** All right, love?

**RITA** See yer later.

## ACT I, SCENE TWO

**RITA** *and the other* **WOMEN** *resume the chanting.*

**WOMEN**  The miners, united, will never be defeated.

The miners, united, will never be defeated.

Say no to bloody blackmail. Say yes to miners' jobs.

## Scene Three

> PHIL *and* SANDRA *at home.* CRAIG *and* MELODY *are fighting. Kylie, in a pram, can be heard crying.*

PHIL  I thought there'd be summat.

SANDRA  If you left me some money there might have been summat.

PHIL  But there's nowt. Bugger all. Frig-all in friggin' fridge. Except friggin' light.

SANDRA  Phil! The kids.

PHIL  What?

SANDRA  Just watch your friggin' mouth, that's all.

PHIL  I would if I had summat to put in it. What's this? This all we got? Friggin' Farley's friggin' rusks? Jesus. I were better off when I were in friggin' prison.

SANDRA  We were all better off when you were in friggin' prison. Hey! What are you doing with them rusks? Don't you bloody dare, Phil. Them's Kylie's.

PHIL  I know. I were just bringing them for her, weren't I? Friggin' hell, what kind of a bloke do you think I am?

SANDRA  *(after a beat; she knows what she could say)* Phil. It can't be meant to be like this.

PHIL  I'm hungry. I've done a shift and I've not had frigging nowt all day.

SANDRA  An' I've been locked up here all day wi' kids yelling and fighting and I've not had frigging nowt neither!

SHANE  Haven't we got owt for our tea, Mam?

SANDRA  There's never been nowt, Shane, and there never will be while I've got breath in me body. You kids'll not go hungry.

PHIL  I will make it right. I love you.

## ACT I, SCENE THREE

**SANDRA** *(not altogether harshly)* Ay, well, look what that leads to... *(She means Kylie)* Phil, gi' us some money?

**PHIL** I'm skint, love.

**SANDRA** Phil!

**PHIL** I can let you have a couple of quid. It's band tonight, subs are due. *(He hands over some coins)*

**SANDRA** Band's more important than feeding kids, then?

**PHIL** No! But...it's not as if I spend it on owt else.

**SHANE** Mam, why are we so poor?

**SANDRA** Ask your father.

**SHANE** Dad...

**PHIL** It's since I were in trouble over strike, Shane, but I'm working regular and I'm paid regular and it'll be all right. Gonna give yer dad a hug?

**SHANE** Don't be soft, Dad. Dad, can I practise me penalties against yer out back?

**SANDRA** Yeah, go on, it saves me practising penalties against yer.

*They start to go.*

**PHIL** *(as they go)* Don't forget I played against David Seaman as a kid.

**SHANE** Yes, Dad, we know. *(To the audience, as he steps out of the "house" with a football)* Sometimes you just have to find summat to do wi' 'em.

## Scene Four

*The street.*

**RITA**, *on her way from* **WOMEN**'s *picket, crosses with* **VERA**.

**VERA**  Hiya!

**RITA**  Hiya! *(To other* **WOMEN**, *if we have any)* See you later.

**VERA**  Good turnout, love?

**RITA**  Not bad. I think it's the only time I talk to Harry now. And all I ever say is "the miners/united/will never be/defeated". Not much of a conversation, is it?

**VERA**  You should hear what I say to Jim sometimes. United isn't in it. Knotted, maybe. Like me new rug?

**RITA**  That'll be foreign, will it?

**VERA**  IKEA. It's lovely up there, Reet. You should come with us. Lovely little cafe and everything.

**RITA**  I don't know, Vera...

**VERA**  You could miss one day on picket. There's other women down there. I'll get you a catalogue...

**RITA**  Vera, *(she refers to the rug)* it's lovely but I don't know if it's us, somehow.

**VERA**  Oh, come on, I'll do you a deal. I'll come down to picket one day if you'll come to IKEA with me.

**RITA**  All right, you're on. I've only got another week up there, any road. Ballot next week. You heard Barmston's taken the money?

**VERA**  Yes, love. *(She pauses)* Band practise tonight, in't it? Is Harry going to resign tonight, then?

**RITA**  Harry will if Jim will.

**VERA**  Jim will if Harry will.

## ACT I, SCENE FOUR

RITA  They never do nowt by theirsens. It's not as if it's any use.

VERA  No, but thing is, Rita, if band goes and pit goes, they'll be under us feet all day.

RITA  No, love, we'll be out at work all day! They'll be the ones choosing fancy rugs! But pit in't going to close, is it?

VERA  I've got quite used to having the house to mesen. And what'll they do if they haven't got band? Spend all the money they're saving in band subs down boozer. And at least you know what they're up to when they're at band. Can't get into much trouble when you've got yer hands full of tuba.

RITA  Eh, up, here they come, the two musketeers.

> JIM *and* HARRY, *benevolently puddled after four quick pints, march home together as they do after every shift of their lives.*

JIM ⎫
HARRY ⎬ *(together)*  Oreight, love?

RITA  *(sotto voce to* VERA*)* Grub on table, is it?

HARRY  Grub on table, is it?

RITA  All ready for yer.

VERA  *(to* RITA*)* I might just have forty winks first.

JIM  I might just have forty winks first.

VERA  Go on, get in. It's there when you want it.

> VERA *exits after* JIM *and* HARRY.

RITA  We could take conversation classes.

> RITA *exits.*

## Scene Five

*The street.*

**SHANE** *addresses the world.*

**SHANE**  They're all watching friggin' Neighbours. All over Grimley. All over Yorkshire. All over world probably. Boring. I hate it.

**ANDY**, *carrying a snooker cue in its case, enters in a hurry and overtakes* **SHANE**.

Hey! Neighbours fan, are you?

**ANDY**  Am I bol–no, I'm not, I'm going for me tea.

**SHANE**  Have you been playing snooker?

**ANDY**  Yes.

**SHANE**  Did you win?

**ANDY**  No.

**SHANE**  Playing Simmo?

**ANDY**  Yes.

**SHANE**  D'you ever beat him?

**ANDY**  Sometimes, yes.

**SHANE**  Will you teach me?

**ANDY**  How old are you?

**SHANE**  Nine.

**ANDY**  You're not, you're eight.

**SHANE**  I can still learn.

**ANDY**  You're not big enough to reach over table.

**SHANE**  On a little table.

**ANDY**  Have you got a little table?

## ACT I, SCENE FIVE 13

**SHANE** I'm saving up for one. Is that your cue? Can I see it?

**ANDY** Shane, me mam's got me tea on table. I'm home for that, then I've just got time for one more game with Simmo, double or quits. Then band.

**SHANE** All go, in't it? *(He grabs the cue case)* Come on.

**ANDY** *(taking back the case, grudgingly getting the cue out)* Oreight...

**SHANE** *(taking the cue from **ANDY** and starting to mime a shot)* I want to be world champion.

**ANDY** Do yer?

**SHANE** At Crucible.

**ANDY** *(crouching behind **SHANE** so that he guides the "shot" with each hand)* I just had to cut the black, ever so thinly, into middle pocket, and I'd have had him. Me favourite shot. Soooo delicate.

**SHANE** What happened?

**ANDY** I missed bugger. Maybe you should get Simmo to teach you.

**SHANE** He won't. I already asked him.

**ANDY** Oh. Right.

**SHANE** I'd rather it was you, though. Is it true you've slept with every girl in Grimley?

**ANDY** You cheeky sod.

**SHANE** Twice?

**ANDY** No!

**SHANE** Not twice?

**ANDY** Give us us cue. I'm going home. Kids!

**SHANE** See yer.

**ANDY** Not if I see you first!

ANDY *goes, fast as he can.*

SHANE *looks after him before turning to us and then his own home.*

SHANE  Still living with 'is mam at twenty-five. It's sandwiches at our house. Me auntie Vera's stale bread she can't sell.

SHANE *exits.*

JIM *and* HARRY *appear with instruments.* RITA *is heading home from a meeting, bearing leaflets.*

RITA  Harry! Harry! Here–take some of these leaflets to band practise with yer and are you resigning tonight, then?

HARRY  Yes, love.

RITA  The both of you?

HARRY  Oh ay.

RITA  Pigs might fly.

RITA *goes.*

JIM  *(reading)* "Say no to bosses' bribes. Fight for your community's future".

HARRY  How long've we been fighting, Jim?

JIM  She's dedicated, your lass. You're a lucky man, Harry.

HARRY  Ay. So what do we say, when Danny comes round for subs?

JIM  Sorry, Danny, but me and Harry have thought about it—

HARRY  No, Jim, thought it through. Folk always say thought it through.

JIM  Sorry, Danny, but me and Harry have thought it through—

HARRY  Nice!

JIM  —and we've got to tighten belts, spend us money on essential items only in present economic climate.

**HARRY**  And band's not one of the aforementioned essential items.

**JIM**  Right.

**HARRY**  Right. And then we wake up in casualty.

**JIM**  No…what can he do? If Danny dun't like it, bollocks to him.

**HARRY**  Ay…bollocks to him.

>   **DANNY** *cycles by, oompahing away.*

**JIM**
**HARRY** } *(together)*  All right, Danny mate?

>   **DANNY** *waves a greeting but doesn't interrupt his "music" and is off.*

**JIM**  Fifty years between us, down pit. You and me. Scared o' nowt. But when it comes to telling Danny we're packing in band…

**HARRY**  Shitting bloody bricks.

**JIM**  Come on.

>   **JIM** *and* **HARRY** *exit.*

## Scene Six

    SANDRA *is at home, doing sandwiches.*

    PHIL *enters with a trombone in two parts.*

SANDRA  God, I hate stale bread.

PHIL  Friggin' trombone keeps coming apart.

SANDRA  Trombones are meant to come apart, aren't they?

PHIL  Not while you're playing 'em.

SANDRA  Phil? Twenty grand. Why can't we take the money just this once? You could get a new trombone. We could pay everything off. I could kit us all out with our own clothes, not second-hand, you don't know who's worn 'em. There'd be a bit left over if you didn't get another job straight away.

PHIL  Straight away? There won't be no other jobs, Sand. It's pit that keeps rest of Grimley going. Pub, shops, chippie, everybody.

SANDRA  Yes, and it's my bad luck to be married to a hero of eighty-four, locked up for defending the cause of the working man…

PHIL  Don't start, Sand…

SANDRA  Oh, I frigging believe it, that's how sad I am.

PHIL  I can't just take money after all that.

SANDRA  All right, what about all these folk you fought for? Where are they now, eh? When you need 'em. With their holidays in Benidorm…

PHIL  Benidorm's cheap, love.

SANDRA  Not cheap enough for us! What about your dad? He must have a bob or two stashed away, only himself to look after.

PHIL  Sandra, I've got me pride!

**SANDRA** Well, good for you, Phil, 'cos I haven't. I don't wear me own clothes, I don't buy fresh food, I don't know if we've got a roof over us heads—

**PHIL** Look, Sandra, we're all saying "No". Pit won't close, it'll go to review. We'll win 'cos it's full o' coal down there and we'll be back to normal.

**SANDRA** Normal? *(She holds up a plate with a stale sandwich)* This is normal. Phil, please don't be a pillock all your life. Take money, while offer's still there.

**PHIL** *(taking the last sandwich)* Talk about it later, eh? Late for practise.

**SANDRA** You'll still be saying later when we're out on bloody street.

*SHANE enters.*

**SHANE** Mam? Kylie's stopped crying.

**SANDRA** What? Well, good…

**SHANE** No, Mam, it means she's doing other thing. *(He holds his nose)*

**SANDRA** Oh…

**PHIL** And there's always Mr Chuckles. I can do more of that. *(He starts to leave).*

*SANDRA follows, a plate in her hand.*

**SANDRA** Phil, you've got a wife and four kids here. In a house nobody'd buy. Mortgaged to hilt. Building society on us backs. Gas, electric, council tax, water bill…all in glorious bloody red. Loan sharks banging on door for their money. No cash. No prospects. Soon no job. And what are you going to do? You're going to fucking juggle. Well. Juggle that! *(She hurls the plate at him)*

*The plate crashes against a wall just as DANNY pulls up on his bike.*

DANNY  Bit clumsy wi' crockery, your Sandra.

PHIL  Now then, Dad.

>PHIL *climbs on to the luggage rack; they cycle off as* SANDRA *and* SHANE *exit indoors.*

## Scene Seven

*The band room.*

*The band members assemble carrying chairs and music stands.* **HARRY**, **JIM** *and* **PHIL** *help get set up.* **HARRY** *is rehearsing his "statement".*

**HARRY**  Aforementioned items, aforementioned essential items... in the present economic climate...

**JIM**  Ay, very good... We are going to play first though.

**HARRY**  Oh ay.

**PHIL**  Lads.

**JIM**  Phil. Got a leaflet?

**PHIL**  What's this then?

**HARRY**  It's my missus' committee. Don't ask me, I haven't read it.

**JIM**  Union's in wi' bastard Mackenzie tonight. Sitting down wi' 'im. They shouldn't be discussing time o' day wi' 'im.

**HARRY**  It's how they get on telly, Jim.

**JIM**  Ay, Yorkshire Telly's there. Look North. Bastard Mackenzie in his bastard Armani suit. Union's sitting down wi' 'im. Cobbling up some new chuffing deal.

**PHIL**  Somebody's got to shout for our side.

**HARRY**  *(looking at the leaflet at last)* Ay, but does every bugger have to shout at our side?

*When the band is ready – not before –* **DANNY** *enters and takes up position as conductor. Instant attention when he taps the baton. He shouldn't have to speak other than:*

**DANNY**  Floral Dance. From top.

*They play* **"FLORAL DANCE"**. *It seems good to us.*

ANDY *is a late arrival though.*

And PHIL*'s trombone comes apart.*

Pile o' crap. What did Eric Morecambe say? All right notes but not necessarily in right order. Cornets, there are some quavers in there. This is because the composer in his wisdom intended them to be quavers. Right, from bar forty. I want to hear every note crystal clear. Ta ka ta ka ta ka ta ka ta ka ta ka tata. If he'd wanted summat else he'd've written it. Or do you know better, any of yer? Right, fag break for those desperate enough to smoke. And kitty...

DANNY *picks up a tin as "our" players come out in front of the rest for a fag break.* DANNY *turns to* PHIL, *who finds a fiver from somewhere.*

What happened, son?

PHIL  Just fell apart.

DANNY  Ay, well, you're not the only one. Andy—

ANDY  Ay, sorry, Danny, got held up.

DANNY  Andy, I'm privileged that you can fit me and band into your busy schedule. It's what you were like after you got here... all over shop. What's up wi' you lot?

JIM  Danny, we have got other things on us minds.

DANNY  Oh ay. Like what?

JIM  Blimey, Danny, you been on Mars or what?

DANNY  Why?

PHIL  Dad...

JIM  It may have escaped your notice, like, pit's under threat.

DANNY  Ay, and what's that got to do wi' us?

HARRY  Danny...oh, you're right, not a lot.

DANNY  Now listen. All on yer. This is a bad time, I know that. But look what it says here *(pointing to his tie)* "eighteen eighty-one"... Over a hundred years this band's been going. Seven strikes. Three disasters. Two world wars. And one bloody big depression. And every time, band... played...on.

**JIM** Danny, this is biggest disaster o' lot.

**HARRY** Can't have a colliery band wi'out a colliery. Can you?

**DANNY** *(resuming his rounds with the tin)* Listen. We've got national semis coming up in Halifax. And we're capable, I mean well capable, of going through to London for the first time in our history. In over a hundred years. The Albert Hall. I know there's bother at pit. I've been down pit mesen in case some of you have forgotten. There's not many conductors can say that. But that's work and this is music. And long after last P45 and long after last ton o' coal, there will still be music. And if we're remembered, that's only bloody way. Now. Jim? Harry?

**JIM** Danny. Me and Harry, we've been thinking it over like. I know subs aren't much but, you know, present climate an' all that.

**DANNY** What are you saying, Jim? Harry?

**HARRY** Well, me and Jim, we've decided...

**PHIL** Eh up!

*A noise at the back of the hall;* **DANNY** *and the band turn to see a nervous* **GLORIA**, *looking stunning in casual clothes and twisting a flugelhorn in her hands.*

*There is a collective intake of breath.*

**DANNY** Bloody hell, lass. Is that a flugelhorn?

**GLORIA** Yes. Is this the band practise hall?

**JIM** No, love, it's a macramé class.

**GLORIA** Well, yes, I can see it is. I'm... um...in Grimley for work for a bit, staying at the Lantern Hotel, and the landlady said you'd welcome me with open arms if I wanted to play with you.

**JIM** Down, boy, down.

**DANNY** I know it might sound like we need all help we can get, but I'm sorry, love, it's a band rule. No outsiders.

**GLORIA** I understand, except... strictly speaking, I'm not. Not an outsider. I was born in Grimley.

**DANNY** Is that right, love? What's your name?

**GLORIA** Gloria...

**DANNY** Gloria what?

**JIM** Stitz. Gloria Stitz.

*Bandsmen snigger.* **DANNY** *isn't amused.*

**DANNY** Sorry, Jim, I didn't quite catch that. Do you want to share it wi' rest of us?

**JIM** No, Danny. It were nowt.

**DANNY** If you're ashamed of it, don't say it! You were saying, love?

**GLORIA** Mullins. Gloria Mullins.

**DANNY** What... Arthur Mullins' Gloria.

**GLORIA** You're Danny, aren't you. I wasn't sure if you'd still...

**DANNY** Be alive? Oh, just about, love, just about.

**GLORIA** No, I meant, leading the band.

**DANNY** Listen, you lot. Talk about miners. Arthur Mullins. This young lady's grandad. Best bandsman I ever played with. Bravest miner I ever worked with. Truest mate I ever had. Till his lungs packed in in nineteen seventy-nine. Sorry, love. Does anybody object to this young lady sitting in?

**ALL** No.

**DANNY** There y'are, love. Park your ar— find yourself a seat.

*GLORIA looks around but ANDY has already found her a chair.*

**ANDY**  Remember me?

**GLORIA**  Barry? Barry Andrews?

**ANDY**  Andy Barrow.

**GLORIA**  Andy Barrow! You haven't changed a bit.

**ANDY**  You have.

**DANNY**  Now, Jim? Harry? What were you saying?

**JIM**  Er...never mind present climate. Stick together, thick and thin. *(He finds a fiver)*

**HARRY**  Solidarity. Put a fiver in for me, Jim.

*JIM does, grudgingly.*

**DANNY**  What we're about, i'n't it? Now, Gloria. What do you know?

**GLORIA**  I've been practising Calaf's big aria from *Turandot*.

**JIM**  What?

**HARRY**  *Nessun Dorma*, Jim.

**JIM**  Oh ay.

**GLORIA**  I'm a bit wobbly...

**DANNY**  Don't fret pet. Wobbly'll be too good for this lot. OK, everybody? Bring your stand forward, Gloria. Andy, you with us? Still got his mind on that pit. *Nessun Dorma*, Andy. None Shall Sleep!

*They play* Nessun Dorma *by Giacomo Puccini.*  *When it finishes the band applauds* **GLORIA**. *For a nanosecond it looks as though* **DANNY** *might hug her.*

---

* The author recommends the arrangement by Howard Snell for use in the performance. For further information, please see the Music and Third-Party Materials Use Note on page iii.

And she calls that wobbly! Right. That's it for tonight and don't forget it's Saddleworth at weekend. Coach at Collier's Arms. Don't be late, Andy.

*As the band starts to disperse,* DANNY *draws* GLORIA *aside.* ANDY *loiters.*

Hang on a minute, love. Are you doing owt much this weekend?

GLORIA  No.

DANNY  Right. It's Saddleworth.

GLORIA  What's Saddleworth?

DANNY  It's a village in Lancashire just outside Oldham, one of fourteen.

JIM  Dobcross, Diggle, Delph...

HARRY  Uppermill...

PHIL  Greenfield—

DANNY  Contest in each. Marching bands. You can play and march at same time?

GLORIA  Don't know...never tried.

DANNY  Well, there's a cash prize for each contest, so we go for—

ALL  All fourteen!

DANNY  Ay, well, big chance to swell our coffers...

GLORIA  Am I allowed?

DANNY  Don't be soft. You were born here. Don't know if we'll have a uniform that fits you. Are you any good wi' a needle and thread?

GLORIA  I'm not an expert...

DANNY  Well, have a go, love. Now then, there's a young miner here, wants to discuss his future, or summat. See you Friday.

## ACT I, SCENE SEVEN

*DANNY and any other stragglers leave ANDY and GLORIA alone.*

*He offers her a cigarette: she refuses.*

ANDY  Fancy 'aving a drink before bedti... er, get to know lads a bit? They do wine and stuff.

GLORIA  It's been a bit of a day. Another time maybe.

ANDY  Yeah. What brought you back?

GLORIA  In a recent survey nine out of ten Londoners didn't know where Grimley was. No, I made that up. Nobody's ever bothered to ask the question. It means sod all to them. I... well, I wanted to see whether it still meant anything to me.

ANDY  And does it?

GLORIA  Give us a chance! I've only just got here. I have got me work, a little research project. But it's hard to know how long it'll last.

ANDY  Join the club.

GLORIA  Andy... I'm sorry I forgot your name.

ANDY  It's been eleven years. Maybe I wouldn't have recognised you. If I'd seen you in London.

GLORIA  Did you ever think of leaving?

ANDY  Not yet. Well, I am having a bevvy. Can I walk you anywhere?

GLORIA  I've got my little car, but thanks.

ANDY  See yer then.

GLORIA  Very soon. On the coach to Saddleworth.

ANDY  Ay. 'Night, Gloria. Welcome back.

GLORIA  'Night.

*ANDY turns to go.*

Andy? Thanks.

*They exit in opposite directions.*

### Scene Eight

**SANDRA** *is at home, carrying a sick* **MELODY**. *She sits by a table.*

**SANDRA** Come here. Look at you. All arms and legs–just like your dad. Your father as a kid were a great long streak o' nowt! Wrists hanging out of his shirtsleeves. Trousers at half mast. He was clean, though, I'll give 'im that. All your grandad knew about rearing kids was, you had to keep 'em clean. Scrubbed him–he used to come into school red raw. My mate Maureen Reece fancied your dad summat rotten. But he didn't fancy her, though, he fancied me. Good job really else you wouldn't be here. He loved coming round our house. Said it always smelled of baking. His house always smelled of shoe polish. Your grandad cleaned his shoes three times a day. And it were dead quiet, unless your grandad were playing his records. Oompah! Maureen Reece. I see her sometimes. She never speaks.

**RITA** *and* **VERA** *appear on the "street" with shopping.*

**VERA** So did Harry say owt, about how Danny Boy took the news, them chucking band?

**RITA** Didn't come in while midnight, V. Too puddled to speak. What about. Jim? They'll've been together.

**VERA** Same. Came home comatose, then up wi' lark to go on earlies, and never a word in between. Not in English any road. Are yer off to pit gates again, love?

**RITA** Ay, in for me thermos, put shopping away, then up there for two. So? When are you going to come with me?

**VERA** I will do, promise yer. It's not that I don't agree wi' yer, Rita. I think you've done marvellous. I have said I'll go in to Sandra.

**RITA** I'll see you later then.

**VERA** Rita...

RITA  What?

VERA  D'you ever think, what I could do wi' that money? You must think o' money sometimes, Rita?

RITA  I don't let mesen, V.

VERA  You could go to Australia and see your Kevin whenever you liked.

RITA  Please don't.

VERA  Bring him an' little 'uns over here.

RITA  Vera!

VERA  Sorry, love. Truly, I'm sorry. It's just…

RITA  I'll see you later, V.

VERA  Yeah. *(Upset at having offended her best friend she shouts at* SHANE*)* Shane Ormondroyd! Where are you with that trolley?

VERA *goes to the "house" area where* SANDRA *is waiting with* CRAIG *and* MELODY.

SHANE *comes flying on, "surfing" a shopping trolley.*

Now then, Sandra.

SANDRA  Hiya, Vera, what do I owe you?

VERA  *(with a till receipt)* Think we got everything on your list, between us.

SANDRA *delves in her purse, eventually tips out its meagre contents for* VERA.

SANDRA  You count it, love. More chance of it being right.

VERA  Sorry, Sand, you're a bit short.

SANDRA  Summat'll have to go back. Is that all right? How much am I short?

VERA  One fifty.

SHANE  What about them aeroplane things, Mam?

SANDRA  What things?

SHANE  Them things with wings. *(He turns into a plane)*

SANDRA  Oh…no, love, your mam needs them. Here, can shampoo go back? We'll make do with soap.

VERA  Still sixty p, love. Tell you what, give it us next week.

SANDRA  Won't it make your till wrong?

VERA  Tell you what will be tricky…if this trolley doesn't get back. He'll have me guts for garters. Here, Concorde! Can you take this back for me?

SHANE  'Course I can.

*SHANE zooms off with the trolley.*

*VERA waits till he's gone then wraps a five pound note in the till receipt.*

VERA  I didn't give you your receipt, love.

*VERA turns and exits fast.*

SANDRA  *(holding up the note)* Vera… Oh, Phil. I don't want to be pitied.

*SANDRA goes.*

## Scene Nine

**PHIL**, **JIM** and **HARRY** *are in the pithead showers, wrapped in towels.* **RITA** *and "Women Against Pit Closures" take up positions in the background.*

PHIL  Christ, they must really want this pit shut.

JIM  There you are. Born bastards, stay bastards.

**ANDY** *arrives late, also in towel.*

ANDY  What's happened?

JIM  It must be for Andy they do the main points of the news again at the end. He's never there at start.

PHIL  They've increased offer. It's gone up from twenty grand to twenty-three if we accept next week, but if we don't–if we vote to stay put and it goes to review–they pull it back down to a flat fifteen.

JIM  Twenty-three grand. Got to hand it to them. Bastards, but clever bastards.

ANDY  But it's profitable, in't it, Grimley? Even the newspapers say so.

JIM  Makes money hand over fist.

PHIL  They really want it shut. Well, we'll tell 'em, bollocks to 'em.

HARRY  Will we?

JIM  Harry?

HARRY  I don't think we will say bollocks to 'em. Twenty-three grand? There's a lot you could do with that.

ANDY  But I don't know anybody who's going to vote to accept.

HARRY  No, and I don' t know anybody who admits to voting Tory but buggers keep getting in.

**PHIL** Yeah, but we don't have to do what the bastards want, do we? We didn't in nineteen eighty-four. We dug us heels in then and some of us got bloody locked up an' all.

**HARRY** Phil, that were ten year ago.

**PHIL** I know it were ten year ago. Suspended I were. Year and a half it took bloody union to get me reinstated. Two and a half years of no wages. Wife, mortgage, kid on way… I were that broke I'm still bloody paying.

**HARRY** Ay and you were a hero in nineteen eighty-four but we still bloody lost.

**PHIL** Well, maybe more on us shoulda got stuck in. Not everybody were on line every day, were they, Harry?

**HARRY** Meaning what?

**PHIL** Your missus's got more bollocks than you have.

**HARRY** Right, you mad bastard…

**PHIL** Any time…

*JIM and ANDY intervene as they rush at each other.*

**JIM** Come on, you're just doing what they want. Besides, if you start wrestling in the nude we'll all get bloody locked up. I'd remind you two that you're supposed to be on same side. Do yer fighting in ballot next week.

**RITA** and **WOMEN** The miners, united, will never be defeated.

*GLORIA is picked out by a light at her desk, on the phone.*

**GLORIA** I'd like to speak to Mr Mackenzie, please. Ms Mullins, Viability Survey… Yes, I'll hold. *(She might hum along with whatever music Mackenzie has on his phone: maybe a tinny speeded-up version of **"BEETHOVEN'S FUR ELISE"**)* Oh, Mr Mackenzie, Ms Mullins–yes, Gloria, that's well remembered! Anyway, just provisional figures so far, but I thought you'd want to know the direction they're taking us. There's plenty of coal there. Ninety years– email? Yes, of course. And you'll get the final ones as soon as they're ready. Good—

*But he's gone. She dials again.*

Right, getting there. Now, uniform. Danny? Gloria. I'm fine. It's the uniform. I can manage the skirt on my own but the jacket's a professional job, isn't it? Shall I give you my measurements?

**RITA and WOMEN** The miners, united, will never be defeated.

**PHIL** I apologise, Harry. There was no call to say what I said. You're a good union man.

**HARRY** Forget it, Phil. No good fighting between oursen.

**RITA and WOMEN** The miners, united, will never be defeated.

The miners, united, will never be defeated.

**ANDY** Poor old biddies. Don't they know they're pissing in the wind like the rest of us?

**HARRY** Can they do that? Women?

**ANDY** Piss in the wind?

**JIM** No, Harry, they can't. That's just the point. Nobody can.

**HARRY** No, but women, even on a nice day, you know, when there's no wind about, women can't get any direction on it. Not like we can.

**JIM** Thanks for biology lesson! All right, whatever lasses can do that's completely bloody pointless.

**ANDY** Bloody hell, spoilt for choice.

**PHIL** Fart in a force ten?

**JIM** By 'eck, Phil, you know some funny women.

**HARRY** My missus does that.

**JIM** What? Fart in a force ten?

**HARRY** No, you daft bastards. She's a woman against pit closures. Pint, lads?

**PHIL** Not me this time, Harry. See you on coach tomorrow? For Saddleworth?

**HARRY** Andy? Or have you got to go and lose at snooker?

**ANDY** I'm just coming into form, lads. See yer tomorrow.

*All start to leave,* **PHIL** *and* **ANDY** *in different directions from* **JIM** *and* **HARRY**.

**RITA and WOMEN** The miners, united, will never be defeated. The miners, united, will never be defeated. Say "no" to bloody blackmail, say "yes" to miners' jobs.

**HARRY** Oreight, love?

**RITA** See yer later.

**HARRY** Only time we ever talk is that.

**JIM** Me and thee against the world then, Harry.

**HARRY** I wouldn't have it any other way, Jim.

## Scene Ten

*The morning of Saddleworth.*

**DANNY**, *bright and early, polishing his shoes and humming the first few bars of Slaidburn.*

**DANNY** Saddleworth, Arthur. Remember when we went there when we were only a fourth section band. Ha! We were only in fourth section 'cos there weren't any more sections! We had basses that sounded like a bulk delivery of syrup of figs. Cornets playing about one note in every four that were written. Ay, we weren't best band in land, but we were loudest! You'd be proud o' band we've got now, Arthur.

**DANNY** *goes.*

### Scene Eleven

SANDRA *enters, dressed up for going out, cheap-smart, sexier than we've seen her.* PHIL *is in desperate pursuit. Kids trail behind.*

PHIL  You can't, love, not today. It's Saddleworth.

SANDRA *sets her face and ignores him.*

We're fighting for band's future, love. Fourteen prizes. Me dad'll kill me if I don't go.

SANDRA  Your dad'll kill you if you don't go. And I'll kill you if you do. Isn't life just shit, Phil? Give us some money.

PHIL  But, Sand, Saddleworth!

SANDRA  Sod Saddleworth! We agreed this.

PHIL  You could go tomorrow.

SANDRA  Me mam's here in two minutes. Phil, you have eight hours away from all this every day.

PHIL  I'm down pit!

SANDRA  That's your choice.

SHANE  Mam!

SANDRA  If I don't have a day away, on me own, I'm going to go frigging barmy. I'm gonna kill somebody.

PHIL  No, love, you don't mean that.

SHANE  Mam!

SANDRA  I just want some peace. You fight for band, Phil. You fight for pit. I'm fighting for family. Only I'm tired. I'm off today, right? I'm off today or I'm off for good.

SHANE  Dad!

SANDRA  I'm gonna do a bit o' shopping, maybe have summat to eat somewhere there's no smell o' nappies and no fighting and no sick on me clothes and no loan sharks at the door; then I'll come back. Give us some money.

**PHIL**  I've only got a tenner.

**SANDRA**  Tenner'll do.

**SHANE**  D'you want a sweet, Mam?

**SANDRA**  Shut up, Shane!

**PHIL**  Don't take it out on kids.

**SANDRA**  You want to please everybody, Phil, everybody 'cept me. Well, this time, I'm pleasing myself.

> **SANDRA** *goes.*

**PHIL**  Sand!

**SHANE**  Dad, what are loan sharks?

**PHIL**  Get in the house, Shane. What've we got for breakfast? Postman Pat spaghetti!

**SHANE**  Dad, I'm eight and a half now.

**PHIL**  Then you'll be able to find the bastard tin opener, won't you?

> **SHANE** *runs out–not after* **SANDRA**.

Oh, Shane, come on…

> **PHIL** *follows* **SHANE** *off with other kids trailing.*

### Scene Twelve

*JIM and HARRY emerge in band uniform and clutching large brass instruments and trying to look inconspicuous; especially when RITA and VERA enter from the opposite direction.*

RITA  Where the hell are you going?

HARRY  We fancied a round of golf like.

VERA  You daft gawpheads. You never resigned, did you? Sat there like a couple of old biddies and paid over money.

JIM  Danny Boy talked us round, pet. He were very persuasive. We had no option, honest.

RITA  No bollocks more like.

*The men walk on. We hear a drain-like laugh from them as they disappear.*

VERA  Look at 'em, two big soft kids...

RITA  No, but look at this, V...

*GLORIA arrives in her band uniform, the skirt a little short.*

GLORIA  Can you help me? Where's the Colliers' Arms?

VERA  Hanging off his shoulders, duck.

GLORIA  *(politely)* The old ones are the best ones, eh?

VERA  It's young 'uns we worry about.

RITA  That way, left, then right and right again.

GLORIA  Oh, that one. Thanks a lot.

VERA  Hey, love. Off to Saddleworth, are you?

GLORIA  Yeah, that's right.

VERA  Just joined band, have you?

**GLORIA**  Yeah. How did you know that?

**VERA**  Summat me husband never said.

> **GLORIA** *walks off after the men.*
>
> *A pause.*
>
> Ay, I am.

**RITA**  What?

**VERA**  Thinking what you're thinking. Come on!

> **RITA** *and* **VERA** *dash off in the direction of home.*

## Scene Thirteen

> **DANNY** *enters with a clipboard, checking off band members in uniform as they board the coach to Saddleworth. Some "real" band members add to numbers he ticks off.*

> **PHIL** *arrives carrying his gaffer-taped trombone and gathering his children.*

**SHANE**  There's Grandad!

**DANNY**  Oh, tell me you're bloody joking, son. Please.

**PHIL**  Sorry, Dad. It's all of us or none at all.

**DANNY**  Why, for Christ's sake?

**PHIL**  Anyway, we could do wi' a bit of vocal support. Come on, kids.

> *Kylie starts to cry as* **PHIL** *shepherds* **CRAIG** *and* **MELODY** *towards the bus, but* **SHANE** *stays alongside his grandad.*

> **GLORIA** *is next and* **DANNY** *perks up no end.*

**DANNY**  By 'eck, lass, hope you feel as good as you look.

**GLORIA**  Nervous…

**DANNY**  Get away. Your grandad would be proud of you.

> **JIM** *and* **HARRY** *materialise bulkily either side of* **GLORIA**.

**HARRY**  Coming to sit with us on back seat, love?

**JIM**  And with this being a colliery band we'd better find you a job while there's time. So, what're your qualifications?

**GLORIA**  Well, *(not comfortable with this)* I'm a surveyor.

**HARRY**  Like a quantity surveyor?

GLORIA  Kind of.

*During the following,* VERA *and* RITA *enter unnoticed, wearing scarves and hats.*

JIM  Well, you could survey my quantity, love.

GLORIA  Well, I do say "No job too small".

*They're still laughing when they look up to see* VERA *and* RITA.

VERA  Don't look like that, boys. These are nearest we could get to band colours. We've formed official fan club. "We had no option, honest".

RITA  We thought you could do with the support, what with men all having soup for brains!

DANNY  Bloody hell. It's Andy! On time!

ANDY *is on time, at a gentle run and carrying a carnation, to match his own, which he presents to* GLORIA, *to a huge chorus of:*

ALL  Whoo-oo!

DANNY  Calm down, calm down. Right, we're going to Lancashire.

ALL  Boo.

DANNY  All right, all right. Now I know for some of you fourteen villages means a chance to have fourteen pints in fourteen different places. Please, please, at least make it halves this time. If we mean business, let's act like it. Right. We're off!

ALL  Yes!

## Scene Fourteen

*Saddleworth.*

*The band forms up offstage.* RITA *and* VERA*, now in charge of the kids, prepare to support them as the taped voice-over of an* ANNOUNCER *is heard, just about audible over an imperfect tannoy, preferably in an East Lancashire accent.*

ANNOUNCER  Is this thing working? It is? Chuffing miracle. Right. Welcome to Diggle Brass Band Contest. Official test piece is *Slaidburn* and drawn number one, Grimley Colliery Band. Grimley first off. Is your mob ready, Mr Ormondroyd?

DANNY  *(offstage)* Ready and willing. One, two…

*The band starts to play* **"SLAIDBURN"** *and march across the stage in good order. A "welcome to Diggle" or a pub sign indicates which village we are in. There is a good opportunity to include the auditorium, foyer and any accessible part of the theatre in this sequence.* RITA, VERA *and the children wave and dance, but as the band passes them* JIM *and* HARRY *peel off the march to join them.* JIM *collects two half pint glasses of beer from offstage and hands them to* HARRY.

JIM  'Ere we are. Just like Danny Boy said. Only halves.

HARRY  Ta, Jim. *(He takes both halves)*

   JIM *fetches two more.*

JIM  Cheers, Harry.

ANNOUNCER  And the winners are…the Cory Band from South Wales. Second, Fishburn, third Bodmin. It's like a geography lesson. And fourth place, Grimley Colliery Band. Grimley fourth.

*The band passes again–new sign saying "Dobcross".* **ANDY** *and* **GLORIA** *are by now noticeably marching together more than may seem necessary for flugel and tenor horns but they continue to play reasonably seriously amid the developing chaos.* **PHIL**'s *trombone comes apart.* **JIM** *and* **HARRY** *join the official supporters club for a group photo.*

And here are the results from Dobcross. First prize, Stalybridge Old Band. Second, all the way from Scotland, Kirkintilloch. Third placed band, Lewis Merthyr. And fifth this time, Grimley Colliery Band. Grimley fifth.

*The band passes a third time, now seriously depleted. A sign bears the name "Delph".* **JIM** *and* **HARRY** *are caught in a light, urinating against a wall, perhaps a box near the stage?* **PHIL** *marches disconsolately on, half a trombone in each hand.* **GLORIA** *has taken one of her shoes off.*

And now the results from Delph...

*The band and their supporters gradually dissolve behind* **DANNY** *who makes his way to the band room where he confronts* **JIM, HARRY, PHIL, ANDY** *and* **GLORIA**.

### Scene Fifteen

**HARRY**  Winners, British Nuclear Fuels. Grimley Colliery Band, seven *(pause)* teenth.

**DANNY**  They were laughing! They were laughing at us. Is this what it's come to? Too bloody bevvied to keep up wi' buggering band. Bits of trombone flying all over the shop. If Arthur Mullins was looking down on us today, God bloody help us. We may as well bloody give up.

**JIM**  I think we already had, Dan. That's kind of why it went like it did.

**HARRY**  Ay. Reckon we thought we'd go out on a high note. Appen our idea of a high note's a bit different to yours.

**DANNY**  What are you on about, "Go out"?

**HARRY**  If pit goes, band goes, dun't it?

**ANDY**  If pit goes…when pit goes.

**GLORIA**  If!

**ANDY**  However ballot goes, they'll still close bugger.

**GLORIA**  Not necessarily. Depends on the…that review thingy, doesn't it? *(She has revealed too much of her knowledge)*

All except **DANNY** *turn to stare at her.*

**DANNY**  Trouble wi' you lot, you've got no pride. What is it more than owt else round here that symbolises pride? This bloody band, that's what. Ask anybody. If they close that pit, bulldoze it flat, fill it in, like they have wi' rest, no trace… years to come, there'll be only one reminder of a hundred years of bloody graft. They've chopped bollocks off unions. They've silenced workers. But they can never shut us up. We'll play on, loud as ever. Louder. Starting at national semis. Win them, we can carry on to Albert bloody Hall. Heads high. Are we playing or are we packing it in?

**GLORIA**  Playing! …Sorry!

**DANNY** You've nowt to be ashamed of, love. No bugger else then?

**JIM** Harry!

**HARRY** Danny... I reckon I speak for all of us. We'll play on while pit's open. As soon as they shut it, we pack it in. You can't ask for more than that.

**DANNY** Obviously not.

*They start to disperse.*

**ANDY** *catches up with* **GLORIA**.

**ANDY** You upset?

**GLORIA** He cares so much.

**ANDY** Ay. Daft old codger. It's what keeps him alive. Listen, do you fancy some grub? Or has it been a bit of a day again?

**GLORIA** It's been a fantastic day! Where?

**ANDY** Spoiled for choice. Chinese takeaway? Kebab? Or we could go posh.

**GLORIA** Let's go posh.

**ANDY** Haddock and chips it is, then.

**ANDY** *and* **GLORIA** *go.*

*The band room is empty now except for* **PHIL** *and* **DANNY** *who has his back to him, coughing his guts up and fighting for breath.*

**PHIL** You all right, Dad?

**DANNY** What? Ta for your support, son. *(He turns, hankie in hands)* Listen, Phil. Semi-finals are no place for scrap metal.

**PHIL** Dad, I'm skint–I can't–I'm not forking out for a new trombone for one performance.

DANNY  One? What about Albert Hall? You're a bloody good trombonist, son. You need, no, you're worth a bloody good trombone.

PHIL  *(after a long pause)* Dad, I like the band—

DANNY *looks up sharply.*

Right, OK, fair enough, I love the band. But there's other things in life. More important things.

DANNY  Not in my life there's not, not any more.

PHIL  Yeah, I know. Dad, there's black on your hankie?

DANNY  Ay. Chain come off on me bike. It's nowt.

PHIL  It'll have to be second-hand.

## Scene Sixteen

*The street.*

**ANDY** *and* **GLORIA**, *eating chips.*

**GLORIA** Well, you certainly know how to show a girl a good time.

**ANDY** This is Grimley, Gloria. What you see is what you get. Can you say same?

**GLORIA** What do you mean?

**ANDY** You're management, aren't you?

**GLORIA** I'm an employee. Same as you.

**ANDY** Fuck.

**GLORIA** I'll tell you what I do. Geological and economic survey. I'm doing a viability study on the future of the pit.

**ANDY** Kept very quiet about it.

**GLORIA** Only 'cos I though you'd get it wrong. And you have. I'm on the same side as you, Andy.

*He laughs.*

Well, I don't know what side you're on, then, 'cos I'm working to keep Grimley pit open.

**ANDY** Gloria, Gloria...they already know pit's viable. In fact it's bloody profitable. But they want to close it anyway. And they will. 'Cos it'll never go to review, whatever they say, 'cos they know the lads'll vote for redundancy. 'Cos the other thing they know–your lot–is just how much to offer to get a result.

**GLORIA** Every miner I talk to is voting to stay put...

**ANDY** As if they'd tell you different.

**GLORIA** What about you?

**ANDY** I'm voting to stay.

**GLORIA** So. Are you lying to me as well?

**ANDY** Of course not.

**GLORIA** So you've got some hope.

**ANDY** No hope, no. Principles…maybe. Is this your first job with them? Course it is. That's why you don't know…your report means about as much to them as we do. Bugger all. Bloody PR exercise. They probably won't even read the bugger. They've already made the decision, Gloria. Probably when you were still at college.

**GLORIA** Oh, don't be ridiculous.

*ANDY lights a cigarette. A silence.*

Andy? Have they pulled the old bus station down?

**ANDY** I didn't think you'd remember.

**GLORIA** How could I forget?

**ANDY** Was I horrible? Fourteen-year-old fumblings.

**GLORIA** I'm embarrassed now. I can distinctly remember…

**ANDY** "Top half only".

**GLORIA** You weren't horrible, Andy. Bit clumsy with the bra strap.

**ANDY** Hadn't had as much practise as I liked to make out.

**GLORIA** Andy, I did remember your name. That first band practice. I was just… It's silly playing games, Andy.

**ANDY** Ay.

**GLORIA** Come back to the Lantern for coffee?

**ANDY** I don't drink coffee.

**GLORIA** I haven't got any.

**ANDY** *(realising)* Ay. All right.

*Blackout.*

*Curtain.*

# ACT II

### Scene One

*The band—or maybe a small section of it—plays a reprise of **"DEATH OR GLORY"**. SHANE is on first, play-conducting. Unlike DANNY who is ramrod straight when he conducts, SHANE begins to move, almost dance, to the music and by the end the band is doing likewise.*

**SHANE** Come on, Grandad. Here y'are.

*DANNY enters, stuffing his handkerchief in his pocket.*

**SHANE** *talks to us first.*

That night, after Saddleworth, I were up later than I'd ever been before. I were stopping over with my grandad. He were still upset. It's his music.

**DANNY** Sithee Shane, music never lets you down. What you put into it, you get out. I used to think it were true o' folk an' all, but not any more.

*HARRY, JIM, VERA and RITA troop on, somewhat the worse for wear, still with instruments, perhaps attempting to play and dance a conga.*

Bloody hell. In boozer all night after a fiasco like that? In Arthur Mullins' day you'd have all been in for extra practise.

## ACT II, SCENE ONE

**JIM**  It were a lock-in, Danny Boy. Held us down and poured beer down us necks. Couldn't get out, honest.

**HARRY**  It were, like, liquid therapy. Getting over trauma.

**VERA**  Shane Ormondroyd, what you doing up so late?

**SHANE**  I'm cheering up me grandad.

**VERA**  It's... *(She peers at a distant clock)* what's the clock say?

**RITA**  It's...half past summat.

> **SHANE** *positions himself for the falling game; in front of* **DANNY** *with his back to him.*

**SHANE**  Catch me, grandad.

**DANNY**  Right. Ready.

> **SHANE** *topples slowly back* **DANNY** *catches him at once.*

**SHANE**  No!

**DANNY**  What've I done wrong?

**SHANE**  You have to let us fall further than that. I don't get the feeling here *(he indicates his stomach)* if it's as quick as that.

**DANNY**  Right. Try again.

*They do. It's better.*

**SHANE**  Better, grandad. See, you have to feel as though you might fall and hit your head.

**JIM**  Sounds like you have fallen and hit your head, young Shane. Playing a daft game like that.

**RITA**  Leave him alone, it's only like that bungee jumping.

**HARRY**  When've you been bungee jumping?

**RITA**  Oh, me, I've never been nowhere, me.

**VERA**  Come on, then. Let's do it now!

**JIM**  What! Bungee jumping?

**VERA**  No, gawphead. This game of Shane's.

**JIM**  It's dangerous.

**VERA**  You. You never let yourself go, do yer?

**JIM**  I do! I've let mesen go tonight.

**HARRY**  He's let go as a newt.

**RITA**  Harry?

**HARRY**  What?

**RITA**  Catch us.

**HARRY**  No, love.

**RITA** / **VERA**  *(together)* Catch-us. Catch-us. Catch-us.

**JIM**  Bloody hell. Come on, then.

**HARRY**  Come on.

*They aren't keen, but they have a go. The* **WOMEN** *don't fall far enough.*

**DANNY**  Nay, that's not far enough. You won't get the feeling. That's right, in't it, Shane?

**SHANE**  Right, Grandad.

**RITA**  Here, let's swap.

**JIM**  What?

**VERA**  Yeah. Me with Harry. Rita with you.

**JIM**  Vera!

**RITA**  Don't worry, Jim, it's only a game. It's not for life. *(To* **VERA***)* It's not, is it?

**VERA**  Up to you, love. He is house-trained. More or less. Come on.

**HARRY**  Come on.

*Another go. They're getting quite good.*

**JIM**  Right, do we get a go?

**RITA**  You what?

**JIM**  Yeah. Equal rights.

**HARRY**  Well, I don't know about that.

**VERA**  Come on, then. I'm ready.

**HARRY**  I never really fancied bungee jumping.

**RITA**  Go on. Give it a go.

**JIM**  One, two, three.

*They try.* **RITA** *ducks away at the last minute.* **VERA** *can't hold* **HARRY**. *All fall down, squealing.*

Rita, where were you?

**RITA**  I forgot.

**DANNY**  Go on, get off home, you lot. Can't practise E flat bass with a hangover, Harry.

**DANNY** *takes* **SHANE** *home.*

**HARRY**  We'll practise on way home, before we get us hangover.

**RITA**  Harry, you'll wake the whole bloody street up.

**HARRY**  Oh. We'll just have to take us shoes off then, won't we!

**VERA**  Take your shoes off! Take your shoes off!

**RITA**  Take your shoes off!

*They do, and all exit, still tooting. But* **RITA**, *in an abstracted dance of her own, follows* **JIM**, *and* **VERA** *follows* **HARRY**. *Offstage there is a terrible scream and the* **WOMEN** *run back on. As they cross...*

**VERA**  Bloody hell, Rita!

*They run off in the right direction at last.*

## Scene Two

*Lights up on post-coital* **ANDY** *and* **GLORIA**.

**GLORIA**  Better than the bus station?

*No reply.*

Andy! Didn't you enjoy it?

**ANDY**  I think you know I did. It was a bit more than enjoyment. That's the trouble.

**GLORIA**  If it was good, what's the problem? Is there somebody else?

**ANDY**  Gloria Mullins, couldn't you have come back as a… hairdresser or summat?

**GLORIA**  Is that it? Andy, why is it a crime that I want to do a bit with my life? Look, I left Grimley when me dad got that college job, the year of the strike. But I'd've wanted to make something of myself. See if I could make a difference.

**ANDY**  Ay, well, you made a choice, I made a choice. 'Cept that it never felt like a choice to me, just felt like…you leave school, you go down pit. I think I do quite an important job. I did, any road. I've got band. I've got spending money.

**GLORIA**  Is that enough?

**ANDY**  There's nowt wrong with it.

**GLORIA**  I didn't say there was.

**ANDY**  And I've got mates. Who've never let me down. And who I've never let down.

**GLORIA**  Yes. I respect that. I'm sort of doing the same, aren't I? And I've tried to strengthen myself so I could help people better.

**ANDY**  Oh, you've strengthened yourself—

**GLORIA**  Andy…look at me… We made love.

ANDY  It was all right, wasn't it?

   GLORIA *nods vigorously.*

   I'm just saying… I don't question you're sincere. Maybe you're not on their side. No, I know you're not. But you're up there, I'm down on bottom rung–and due for scrap heap at twenty-five. I don't know if your kind of "helping" …helps. And I do think you're naïve. And in some ways I wish this was the old bus station and we were still in the same class.

GLORIA  You're not asking me if there's anybody else, I notice.

   ANDY *shoots her a stricken look.*

   There isn't. Do you want to go–look at me–do you want to go?

ANDY  No.

GLORIA  Don't go yet. You've got a bruise, little boy.

ANDY  Lump o' coil, love. Near miss.

   *She pulls him down.*

## Scene Three

> **PHIL** *as Mr Chuckles is trying out a card trick with* **SHANE** *at home.*

**PHIL**  It was the ace of diamonds.

**SHANE**  Was not.

**PHIL**  Was.

**SHANE**  Not.

**PHIL**  Weren't it?

**SHANE**  No. It were a black one.

**PHIL**  Sod it. Where's the book?

**SHANE**  No, leave it, Dad. Kids'll laugh. They see magic working all the time on telly. You can fake things on telly, can't yer? You want to be different.

> **SANDRA** *enters to overhear this. She is taking advantage of a Sunday morning lull to wander around with a coffee, a fag and a magazine (all from her day out with her mother). This is the most relaxed we see them.*

**SANDRA**  Oh, he'll be different, all right. Is someone going to pay you for that?

**PHIL**  Why shouldn't they? It's hard to get live entertainment for kids. I'll be in a sellers' market. Make us a fortune.

**SANDRA**  Poor little mites. Won't be able to get away. You'll frighten the life out of 'em. You do try, Phil, I'll give you that.

**PHIL**  Eh, give us a kiss.

**SANDRA**  Sod off!

**PHIL**  Go on.

**SANDRA**  Won't be the first time I've kissed a clown. *(She does)*

> **SHANE** *winces.*

SHANE  Disgusting. Dad? When will I be grown up?

PHIL  When you leave school I suppose. Why?

SHANE  I want to see what happens.

PHIL  Do yer?

SHANE  To me brain. Our teacher, Mrs Robinson, says I've got quite a good brain if I'd only use it. But I heard Auntie Rita say to Auntie Vera that all men had soup for brains. So I was wondering what'd it be like when me brains turned into soup.

PHIL  Er… I think I'll practise me juggling. *(he does)*

SANDRA  I think I'll get dressed.

SANDRA *goes.*

SHANE  You could play 'em your trombone, Dad. It could come apart, like it did at Saddleworth. That'd make 'em laugh. Unless you got that one in White's second-hand shop.

PHIL *drops a ball.*

PHIL  How d'you know about that?

SHANE  Uncle Jim and Uncle Harry said. They found you outside White's second-hand shop. At midnight. Gawping at trombone behind plate glass. They said you had a coat wrapped round your arm, like. I've seen that on telly.

PHIL  Seen what?

SHANE  You wrap coat round yer arm if you're gonna smash glass. Stops you getting cut.

PHIL  I were only looking.

SHANE  What's "nostalgic", Dad?

PHIL  When you want things to be like they were.

SHANE  Uncle Jim said you were nostalgic for Armley jail.

## Scene Four

**GLORIA** *at work, reading a letter.*

**GLORIA** "Dear Ms Mullins, Thank you for your query. I am truly sorry that you have experienced some difficulty in getting statistical information…blah di blah… I want to reassure you personally, Ms Mullins, that your report is absolutely vital and will be treated with the greatest seriousness. If Grimley goes to review as, believe me, we all hope it will, we shall have crucial decisions to make. And we can't make them without detailed, accurate reports from highly qualified people such as yourself. Blah di blah, yours sincerely, Colin Mackenzie, Manager, Grimley Colliery." See, Andy Barrow? You're being paranoid. But very tasty.

## Scene Five

*The colliery ballot, a big metal box on a table.*

*In turns* **HARRY**, **PHIL**, **ANDY**, **JIM** *and men from the band pick up a ballot paper, put a cross on it, fold it... and then walk to the ballot box. As they drop their papers in they all thump the top of the box in case the ballot paper sticks in the opening, somebody pulls it out and reveals how they've voted. There could be music behind this steady repeated action, either tape or a soloist or small group from the band probably in elegiac mode. We hear* **VERA** *and* **RITA**'s *muted chanting occasionally.*

**VERA** and **RITA**  The miners, united, will never be defeated. The miners, united, will never be defeated.

**HARRY**, *after casting his vote, takes a position apart from the rest. Other soliloquys follow at intervals, with music and men voting in between. As each man votes he folds the ballot paper, places it in the box and then thumps it to make sure it drops in.*

**HARRY**  Elephants. Such big buggers. They stare at you as if they know everything. Like God. Maybe they do. Look sad enough. With me dad it was having a little white sports car. Allus dreamed of it, never got it. Me an' Jim do just about everything together. Booze, band, Benidorm. Your mates... it's like gold dust. But I've wanted to see elephants since I were a kid. Not behind bars. I just want to go to Africa before I die and talk to an elephant.

**VERA**  Twenty-three grand. Oh, I know it's not much, not really. But spend it on yer home, you could have a little palace. I know I'm nowt special. You know what they say about the likes of us: put on earth to make the numbers up. And we never had no kids. They just never came. But I could make a home, I know I could. Somewhere folk'd look at and say, that's Vera's place. They could just tell. And Jim's of course.

**RITA** Money's not that much but Vera's right. I'd be on first plane to see our Kevin and kids if I had it. Here I am campaigning for pits to stay open but every day of my married life I've hated Harry going down there. Not one of us says owt, even to the men, but not one of us doesn't pray every day, please God, just let him come home today, in one piece. I never wanted Kevin to go down. But why did he have to go all way round world to do summat else?

**JIM** Twenty-three grand. It's fucking peanuts when you come to think about it. Invest it, and what'll you get. Twenty pound a week? Thirty, top whack. That bastard Mackenzie'll spend that much on one bottle of wine in a fancy restaurant. And my little Vera, who thinks she's nowt but is just a better person than any on 'em, she thinks twenty-three grand is a little pot of gold!

*There is one last chorus from the* **WOMEN**, **RITA** *and* **VERA** *now with arms linked.*

**RITA AND VERA** The miners, united, will never be defeated. The miners, united, will never be defeated.

*Music finishes and so does the ballot.*

**HARRY**, **JIM**, **ANDY** *and* **PHIL** *regroup as the stage empties.*

## Scene Six

GLORIA *arrives in her work clothes to encounter the men.*

JIM  Hallo, love, what's a nice girl like you doing in an 'orrible place like this?

GLORIA  Hi… I just came to meet Andy out of work.

HARRY  He in't out of work yet, love. Come back next week.

GLORIA  Just wondered if you wanted an extra practise, Andy? Before the semis. Or anyone?

JIM  *(suddenly harsher)* He can't, love. He's going for a pint with us.

GLORIA  Oh…right. See you on the bus then.

GLORIA *exits.*

JIM *turns to the apparently mute* ANDY.

JIM  That's all right, isn't it, Andy? Nice pint and a chat. We can talk about pros and cons of Darren Gough, plight of Third World…and why your bird's got a British Coal logo on her briefcase.

ANDY  It's over, anyway. It were over as soon as I found out.

PHIL  Any road, it dun't make her devil incarnate, does it?

JIM  What does it make Andy, that's what I want to know.

PHIL  Oh, lay off him, Jim, eh? He said it's over with.

HARRY  Hey, with legs like that wrapped round your back you don't stop and ask for a reference, do you?

PHIL  Mistake anyone could've made.

HARRY  I wish I'd made it.

JIM  This in't a joke!

HARRY  Jim, what's wrong wi' shagging management. They been shagging us for years.

**ANDY** Leave it, Harry!

**JIM** Oh don't tell me, Andy. It weren't shaggin' ...it were true love. All together now. Aaaaaaah!

**PHIL** Fuck off, Jim.

*PHIL exits.*

**ANDY** What the fuck would you know about it? I'm playing snooker.

**JIM** *(stopping him)* You've had enough fun and games for one day.

**ANDY** Fuck off, Jim, I'm not a kid.

**JIM** Is that right?

**ANDY** Yeah.

**JIM** Old enough to be a scab, then?

*An awful silence.*

**HARRY** It's all right, Andy, he dun't mean that.

**ANDY** Was that a "joke", Jim?

**JIM** It were a joke, ay. I'm sorry, Andy. I take it back. You're just a stupid fucker.

**ANDY** That's more like it. Right, I am playing snooker.

*ANDY leaves.*

**HARRY** Just thee 'n' me again, Jim.

**JIM** Young 'uns. They weren't beaten in eighty-four. They weren't on winning side in seventy-four. But worst of all they don't understand whose side they're on.

**HARRY** I know, Jim. But I feel a bit for lad. He's never settled. As soon as he finds some lass he really likes he has to pack her in as soon as he's struck lucky.

**JIM** You'll be telling me you're sorry for lass 'n' all in a minute.

**HARRY**  Well, she's not a bad lass. Even you took a shine to 'er an' all when she came into that practise room.

**JIM**  Bollocks, Harry.

*They exit.*

## Scene Seven

**PHIL**, *dressed extravagantly as Mr Chuckles, is walking slowly home in clown's shoes, with* **SHANE** *trailing him; he is trying out a new (to him) trombone.*

*In the house, two bailiff's men confront* **SANDRA** *and the other kids, one writing out a receipt before picking up a television.*

**SHANE**  Dad?

**PHIL**  Seemed to go all right. Kids didn't seem to mind that balloon animals look like no animal known to science. Maybe they're getting their sense of fantasy back.

**SHANE**  Dad!

**PHIL**  What?

**SHANE**  It's 'cos you said "friggin'". That's why they laughed. "Well what does it friggin' look like?" I don't think that lady liked it though.

**PHIL**  Had to pay me, though.

**PHIL** *blows another arpeggio.*

**SHANE**  Dad! D' you want receipt? *(He waves the receipt at* **PHIL***)*

**PHIL** *takes it.*

Trombone took everything she paid you, didn't it?

**PHIL**  Ay, and a bit more. Look, just for now, we' ll keep this between oursens, yeah?

**SHANE**  Like a surprise?

**PHIL**  Yeah, like a surprise.

*But* **SHANE** *has seen men carrying away the telly.*

**SHANE**  Dad. It's them men. They've got our telly! *(He launches himself at the men and is roughly brushed off)*

PHIL *arrives later, due to the clown's shoes.*

SANDRA *arrives with* RITA *and the kids.*

SANDRA  No, Shane, leave it.

PHIL  Take him in house, love. I'll sort this.

SANDRA *and the kids exit.*

PHIL *grabs the heavy by the arm.*

Touch my kids again and I'll fucking kill you. Just give me till next week.

*Very quickly the heavy hits him once, hard.* PHIL *falls, but saves the trombone as best he can.*

*The men exit.*

SANDRA *reappears as* PHIL *gets up.*

SANDRA  Phil!

PHIL  I'm all right.

SANDRA  Are you? What the frigging hell's that?

PHIL  It's a frigging dent, that's what it is. Andy Barrow lent me it. He'll go frigging barmy.

SANDRA  Andy Barrow? What's he doing with a trombone?

PHIL  Come on. If I'm going to make a spectacle of mesen I might as well get paid for it.

*They go indoors, except for* SHANE.

## Scene Eight

SHANE  Day of semis in Halifax and me mam were ominously silent. It was also day they were due to announce results o' pit ballot. Both about five o'clock an' all. Just when football results come in.

*SHANE remains on stage as an observer until called indoors by his mother in Scene Ten.*

*JIM and HARRY come out of houses in uniform just as RITA comes the other way with her thermos.*

Close-knit community's strangely at odds.

HARRY  All right, love?

RITA  Oh go and blow your bloody trumpet.

HARRY  Blimey. A conversation.

RITA  Harry. In a month's time when you're at home all day and there's nowt coming in but dole, at least I can say I did summat. Not much, but best I could do and it were summat.

HARRY  I've been to meetings. Before ballot.

RITA  You used to be…so full o' fight. Packed full o' passions you were before strike. Now…you're resigned! You…just blow your bloody trumpet.

HARRY  Ay, but at least…

RITA  Go on. Say it.

HARRY  People listen to us.

RITA  *(deeply wounded)* Go on. Sod off.

*RITA exits.*

HARRY  Any road. It's not a trumpet. It's an E flat bloody bass. She knows it's an E flat bass.

JIM *(deeply embarrassed)* Come on, lad. Let's go and find the coach.

### Scene Nine

DANNY *is checking the band members against his clipboard.*

DANNY Jim, Harry!

JIM } *(together)* All right, Danny.
HARRY

DANNY Ay!

GLORIA *arrives.*

Hiya, love! *(But he just gets a tight little smile and his face falls)*

PHIL *arrives with a spectacularly bruised face.*

Oh, Phil, lad, what the bloody hell...

PHIL Sorry, Dad, bit of a domestic.

DANNY You of all people know–what, Sandra? Did that?

PHIL No! Don't worry–they didn't get me lip.

DANNY Well, bang goes deportment prize.

PHIL *goes to board the bus.*

Just the one left, guess who. Fast bloody Eddie. Get a move on, Andy, we'll be late.

ANDY *manages a reluctant trot but otherwise doesn't acknowledge* DANNY *as he passes.*

She'll be sat on her own at front, lad. Rest of band's at back. Try being a human being and see if you can manage half way. Oh, please, God, when we get there, I promise I'll believe in you forever if you can get them to play together. Can't be harder than creating world. Can it?

## Scene Ten

**SANDRA** *is at home, desultorily sorting out clothes for the washing, specifically the Mr Chuckles outfit. In its trouser pockets she finds a piece of paper which she reads.*

**SANDRA**  Shane! Come here!

**SHANE** *drags himself to face her.*

You know anything about this?

**SHANE**  No.

**SANDRA**  You don't even know what it is yet.

**SHANE**  What is it?

**SANDRA**  White's Second-Hand Store. To one trombone: fifty pound received, two hundred and fifty still to pay. Did you see him do this?

**SHANE**  No, Mam.

**SANDRA**  Oh Shane, we've got no money, bailiffs at the door, building society…and he spends three hundred pounds on a sodding trombone. Oh Phil, your kids are hungry, your wife's going mental, but you've got your music so that's all right…

## Scene Eleven

> **SANDRA** and **SHANE** are joined in the "house" by **CRAIG** and **MELODY**. *The band is in "Halifax" which is ideally offstage, perhaps in the foyer with the auditorium doors open so they can be heard as if at one remove.* **DANNY** *is heard speaking to them in voice over, a sotto voce pep talk before this key performance. If it is impossible to take the band offstage, they should at least be completely oblivious to the action at home.*

**DANNY**  Right, I know you buggers are in despair. You can't forget it. So put it in the fucking music. Sorry, but this is probably my last chance. Just fucking do it. If not for me, for yourselves, for a thousand other families. Sorry about language. I'm worked up. Right! Florentina!

*The band starts to play* ***"FLORENTINA".***

*A minute or so in, the bailiffs arrive at* **PHIL** *and* **SANDRA**'s... *A gang of them. Everything worth anything is removed.* **SANDRA** *takes a soft toy back from one of the heavies who shrugs and leaves with his colleagues.*

**SANDRA** *bundles the few belongings they have left into an old suitcase, straps the baby into a buggy and they leave, the image of refugees.*

*The band plays on.*

**RITA** *appears at the pithead with a notice she pins to it.*

**VERA** *follows her on with a large wreath.*

*A moment's silence.* **VERA** *leads* **RITA** *away.*

**ANNOUNCER**  The winners, and the Yorkshire Area Champions, Grimley Colliery Band!

*Cheers from the band dying quickly away.*

RITA  Four to one, V. Our own people. Four to one to close pit. They'll never get it back.

VERA  You fought, love. You did what you could.

*As it starts to get dark,* JIM, HARRY, PHIL, ANDY *and* DANNY *drift on, in celebratory mood.* GLORIA *follows, clearly apart.*

RITA  Harry?

HARRY  Rita love.

RITA  *(close to breakdown)* At least you're alive.

HARRY  I've only been to Halifax, love.

RITA  No, pit. We fought and lost…see a bit more of each other now, eh?

HARRY  Ay, come on.

*They hold each other.* DANNY, *his triumph soured, moves a little way off. Jim goes to* VERA. DANNY *starts to cough, longer and worse than usual. He falls to the ground gasping for breath.*

ANDY  Phil!

PHIL  Dad! Get an ambulance.

PHIL *leads the rush towards* DANNY. *Shouts of "give him air" and "call an ambulance" and maybe the sound of a siren leading to…*

*Blackout.*

## Scene Twelve

*Lights up on the same scene except that* **DANNY** *has gone.* **JIM** *has found the band's kitty tin and is collecting.*

**JIM**  Whip-round for Danny Boy. Andy?

**HARRY** *and* **ANDY** *put money in.* **JIM** *comes to* **GLORIA**.

You still here, love?

**GLORIA** *puts money in.*

Thanks. Reckon it's got to be ta-ra now, don't you.

**GLORIA**  I'm on your side. I always was.

*They all inspect the floorboards.*

Andy...

*They look at each other. Mutual appeal but nothing comes out.*

**GLORIA** *turns, takes her flugel and her bag and leaves in silence.*

**JIM** *holds out the tin to* **PHIL**, *who has no money.*

**JIM**  Phil? You in on this?

**PHIL** *turns out his pockets. Nothing.*

**PHIL**  *(turning to go)* Not flowers, Jim, all right? Not grapes. Don't get him grapes, he can't stand 'em. Get him summat he wants, eh?

*All exit.*

## Scene Thirteen

> **PHIL** *is on his way home when he meets his family.*

**PHIL**  Sand?

**SANDRA**  They came, Phil. Took the bloody lot. I did warn you, Phil.

**PHIL**  Oh, eh, Sand. Not now, eh? Don't...

**SANDRA**  They'll be warm at me mam's. They'll be fed. Just till I get settled.

**PHIL**  Sand. Me dad's collapsed.

**SANDRA**  I am sorry, Phil. It's not that I don't love you no more. You understand that, don't you.

> **PHIL** *is in dumb assent.*

> Bye, Phil.

**SHANE**  Bye, Dad.

> **PHIL** *arrives at the empty house and sinks to the floor.*

## Scene Fourteen

**GLORIA** *enters, angry and carrying her report. The managers she is addressing are not seen.*

**GLORIA**  Grimley Colliery Economic Viability Report by Gloria Mullins, BA and complete idiot. Waste of time, waste of energy. Grimley pit is profitable–says so in my report, but you're never going to read it. Two years you've known you were gonna close the pit, way before the miners voted, way before I was even qualified to do the job. Economic decision to close? I don't think so. You're a bunch of fat, fucking farts. *(After a short pause)* Right. I'll clear my desk.

### Scene Fifteen

**PHIL**, *desolate, is sitting on the floor in an empty house.*

**JIM**, **HARRY** *and* **ANDY** *approach the house carrying instruments.* **ANDY** *is with them, but empty-handed. All have miners' helmets and a spare one for* **PHIL**. **PHIL** *doesn't respond until they are very close, and then dully.*

**HARRY**  Phil?

**JIM**  Phil? Are you there?

**PHIL**  Lads?

**HARRY**  Are you set for one final performance?

**PHIL**  Are you going to tell me what we're doing?

**JIM**  On the way. We've a few others to pick up first.

*They leave.*

**PHIL**  *(to* **ANDY***)* Where's yours?

**ANDY**  Lost it. I had the black right over the pocket. Slam. In it went. Only bastard white followed it down.

**PHIL**  You were betting with your horn?

**ANDY**  Don't worry, mate. I've lost more than a tenor horn this week. Are you fit?

*They join the small section of the band, all in helmets and with lamps switched on, at the back of the stage.*

## Scene Sixteen

*A hospital.*

**DANNY** *is in bed, apparatus for a drip and/or oxygen nearby.*

*The small band starts to play **"DANNY BOY"**. Andy gently croons his part.*

**NURSE VERA**  What the hell...

**NURSE RITA**  I don't believe it!

**NURSE VERA**  A bloody brass band. We'll see about this...

**DANNY**  Leave 'em be!

**NURSE RITA**  Mr Ormondroyd! How are you feeling?

**DANNY**  Death's door. And still the bastards take the piss.

**NURSE VERA**  Don't worry. We'll soon stop this racket.

**DANNY**  Stop this racket, love, and you'll wake up in next ward!

**NURSE VERA**  Well!

> **NURSE VERA** *sticks a thermometer in his mouth and leaves. As soon as she can't see,* **DANNY** *removes the thermometer and starts "conducting" with it. It's just back in his mouth when the music, played with maximum emotion, comes to an end and she returns to take his pulse.*

**DANNY**  Going like shit off a shovel, is it?

**NURSE**  If by that you mean fast, yes, it is rather.

**DANNY**  It's tenor horn's fault. Playing too soft. And they won't be told.

**NURSE**  I know the feeling.

*The members of the band are trooping into the ward.*

*HARRY takes PHIL aside.*

JIM  Eh up, Danny.

HARRY  Phil, lad, reckon it'd be best coming from you. About band packing in now pit's gone.

*As the front of the troop* JIM *hands* DANNY *a present.*

DANNY  You shouldn't have, lads, really. You could've brought some flowers or summat. Grapes, I could murder some grapes.

*PHIL has got something else wrong.* DANNY *unwraps a small box which he opens to discover a gold baton.*

Bloody hell.

*He has to turn away. The* NURSE *takes charge.*

NURSE RITA  Right, thank you, the concert's over. It's past eleven.

NURSE VERA  There's three police vans outside—

HARRY  *(interrupting)* Three! I can remember when it would have taken forty-three!

NURSE RITA  Mr Ormondroyd needs sleep.

NURSE VERA  And I'd prefer any future visits to be in visiting hours and without your bloody trumpets.

JIM  It's a eu-bloody-phonium.

*The bandsmen shuffle off.*

DANNY  Phil, son. Quick word?

HARRY  Tell him, Phil.

*All the others go.*

DANNY  You in a bit of trouble, Phil? You seem upset, like.

PHIL  Course I'm upset. Me old man's poorly.

DANNY  Ay, well, we'll both get over that. Nice bit of brass. *(He fingers, but does not mention, the dent)* You'll have got it cheap, yeah?

PHIL *nods.*

Ta, son. It mattered, you know. To me, any road.

PHIL  Ay, I know. Well, best be off. Get some shut-eye, yeah?

DANNY  Ay. Say hallo to Sandra and kids.

PHIL  Ay. They said…get well soon.

DANNY  Phil, I were alongside Arthur Mullins every day of his working life, you know that? And when they opened him up…

PHIL  Dad, don't…

DANNY  They say, when they opened up his lungs there was nowt in there but coal dust. 'Nough slack to have kept fire in for a week.

PHIL  Dad, you'll be all right.

DANNY  You going to tell lies to your father all night? No, you're right. I'll be out of here in time for final. One way or another.

PHIL  'Night, Dad.

### Scene Seventeen

*The men are at a Job Centre, looking at a board or in a newspaper.*

ANDY  Owtin?

PHIL  Oh ay, machinist wanted. Any good at button stitching?

ANDY  I'll try owt.

PHIL  Good. You can start Monday.

ANDY  How's yer dad?

HARRY  How did he take it when you told him, Phil?

PHIL *hasn't told him.*

Oh hey, Phil, you've got to tell him before finals, man.

PHIL  I'm gonna–they're a while yet though, aren't they?

JIM  Phil, it's next Saturday.

PHIL  Fine, I'll go now then, shall I.

PHIL *exits, furious.*

HARRY  Cashier/cleaner wanted for busy petrol station. Must be honest, hardworking and reliable.

JIM  No chance. Care assistant, two pound ninety-three an hour, must be cheerful and outgoing.

ANDY  You'd have to be fucking cheerful, to live on two pound ninety-three an hour.

HARRY  Security guard, night watchman in't it? Only down here at chuffing pit!

GLORIA *enters.*

*The others turn away, leaving her with* ANDY.

GLORIA  Hiya. I've come to say goodbye, Andy.

ANDY  For years for bloody years, nowt good happened to me. The only reason I get up in morning's to see if me luck's changed and it never has and it was just beginning to get worse, pit closing, losing me job, when what happens? Gloria Mullins, love of my bloody life, walks into practise hall. Hell fire, I thought, maybe life's not so bad after all. Is it buggery? She only turns out to be management.

GLORIA  I'm not anymore. I'm unemployed like you. I told them to stick their stupid job.

ANDY  So, you'll be off back down south, then?

GLORIA  Well, I'm not welcome here, am I?

ANDY  I reckon your heart's in the right place, but you never did nowt to prove it.

GLORIA  I'll say ta-ra then. Summat good'll happen soon, Andy. Let's just hope it's at the Albert Hall.

ANDY  Doubt it somehow. We're not going.

GLORIA  What?

ANDY  They worked it out. It cost three grand or summat. We can't spare that sort of money now. Band's dead. Dead with everything else.

GLORIA  *(shouting so they can all hear)* You're fucking pathetic.

GLORIA *spins and goes.*

JIM  Let's not ask. Time for a wet?

*The others trudge in opposite direction.*

## Scene Eighteen

*The hospital.*

*PHIL is clutching a bunch of grapes.*

*The NURSE intercepts him before he reaches DANNY.*

NURSE  Oh, Mr Ormondroyd. There is a bit of a problem with your father. Nothing serious although of course he is still very ill. It's just... He thinks he's going to London on Saturday. I'm all for him looking on the bright side, it helps him recover, but I'm afraid it's going to be weeks yet. He won't listen to us. Do you think you could...

PHIL  Oh ay, course I could, I can do everything, me...

*NURSE turns away as he arrives at DANNY's bedside.*

Dad. Dad, you've got to listen to me.

*PHIL hands over the bunch of grapes. DANNY barely glances at them before dropping them.*

DANNY  You're gonna tell me I can't be let out, not even for a single day.

PHIL  You're very poorly.

DANNY  Ever since I were ten, since I blew me first note, I've been waiting for a day like Saturday. What's me life worth...?

PHIL  Dad, Dad, it's worse than that. I'm afraid I've got some very bad news...

DANNY  What–Sand and the kids? Oh, I heard all about that. Don't fret, they'll be back. Just one day .They won't let me out for one sodding day...

PHIL  No, well, I suppose they do know best. Dad...eh?

DANNY  *(producing his notes)* Better take these then. Hope you can read them, hand-done like. Took me hours. Give 'em to Harry. It's a really nifty new arrangement. I think the lads'll like it.

**PHIL** *can say nothing. He leaves.*

### Scene Nineteen

SHANE *is in his new Barnsley Number 8 shirt.*

SHANE  Did you see me score, Mam?

SANDRA  Course I did–you were brilliant.

SHANE  Mam, I like this shirt and it's great stopping at Nan's but there's me grandad.

SANDRA  What about your grandad?

SHANE  Dad said, when people are as poorly as me other grandad, you have to do special things for them.

SANDRA  Shane, love, he didn't get trombone for your grandad. He gorrit for himself.

SHANE  He said, Grandad's going to die, but at least Dad gerrin' trombone would make him die happy. Mam?

SANDRA  What?

SHANE  How the 'eck can you die–happy?

SANDRA *hugs him.* SHANE *frees himself.*

Get off, Mam. Mam. I know we've got no money

SANDRA  We're in debt, Shane. We'll never have no money. Everything he gets he'll just have to pay back. Debt's getting bigger, not smaller. And he never told me that. Why wouldn't he do that?

SHANE  Trying not to worry yer?

SANDRA  Not worry me!

SHANE  You've too many kids, haven't yer?

SANDRA  Shane Ormondroyd, ask me which I'd rather have, money or kids. Go on, ask me.

SHANE  Mam, I don't like seeing me dad sad.

SANDRA  No, love.

**SHANE**  But I'd rather see him sad than not at all.

**SANDRA**  Come on, love–inside–it's gerrin' dark, love.

**SANDRA** *and* **SHANE** *exit.*

*It is getting dark.*

## Scene Twenty

*As the pithead winding gear is unnaturally illuminated by the floodlights of the mine,* **PHIL** *climbs to the wheel level.*

**PHIL**  And God was creating Man. And his assistant says, his personal assistant because God's like a colliery manager, important enough to have a personal assistant. His assistant says: "we've got plenty of bodies left but we're right out of hearts and right out of brains and right out of vocal cords". "Dun't matter", says God, he speaks with a Yorkshire accent like. "Dun't matter. Sew 'em up, smack a smile on their stupid faces and they can talk out of their arses". And that, boys and girls, is how God invented the Tory Party. Another one? What do you call a miner with a future? A fucking mirage. Hey, it's the way I tell 'em. Yeah, God. Now there is a feller. What's he playing at? He's thinking of taking my old man and Maggie bastard Thatcher lives! Thank you. You've been great. My name's Coco the scab. Goodnight.

*Cornet solo, maybe muted,* **JERUSALEM**.

**PHIL** *hangs himself. As* **JERUSALEM** *is swamped by the sound of sirens and men shouting, he is briefly picked out in a light, legs kicking and hands scrabbling at his neck.*

## Scene Twenty One

*DANNY in bed reading, NURSES downstage, one looking at clipboard.*

**NURSE VERA**  A miner, apparently.

**NURSE RITA**  Another one. Did he mean it? Or was it a "cry for help"?

**NURSE VERA**  Well, if he didn't mean it, he damn near did it. Another couple of seconds...

**NURSE RITA**  He dressed up in a clown's costume to do it. Ormondroyd...

*They both look at DANNY.*

## Scene Twenty Two

*We hear the last few notes of **JERUSALEM** and a lighting change indicates a new day.*

**DANNY** *is sitting up when* **PHIL** *approaches in a dressing gown.*

**DANNY**  What the bloody hell d'you think you were playing at, son? Lost your marbles?

**PHIL**  'Appen. Lost everything else. Job. Wife. Kids. House. Self-respect. Hope. But then, that's nowt is it, Dad? Cos it's music that matters. Band's packed in an' all.

**DANNY**  *(trying to shout)* Wha'...what did you say?

**NURSE** *comes scurrying.*

**NURSE**  *(to* **PHIL***)* Is this man bothering you, Mr Ormondroyd?

**PHIL**  Course he is. He's me dad.

**PHIL** *and the* **NURSE** *leave.*

## Scene Twenty Three

> RITA *enters with a plant in a pot. She gazes at the label and scratches her head.*
>
> GLORIA *enters with a bunch of tickets, a list of addresses and something to keep cash in.*
>
> RITA *looks at her and then away.* GLORIA *hesitates and then...*

GLORIA  Rita?

RITA  Know owt about gardening?

> GLORIA *shakes her head.*

RITA  Me neither.

GLORIA  Look... I'm selling tickets door to door. Trying to. I need help. Do I need permission from Arthur Scargill?

RITA  Don't joke about Arthur, love. Not while you're an outsider. We can. You can't. No offence like. What's these tickets, then?

GLORIA  Coach trip to London, band contest at Albert Hall.

RITA  Are they going?

GLORIA  Only if we make 'em. It's for Danny, Rita.

RITA  *(after a pause)* Ay. All right. We'll get Vera on this when she finishes work. She's a right saleswoman.

GLORIA  Is she? Jim's not me number one fan.

RITA  No, love, but he's a man and what the eye dun't see the heart dun't grieve over. What's this deal then?

GLORIA  House to house, we offer 'em four tickets for the price of three.

RITA  Seems fair. Sometimes men just go their own way and there's bugger all you can do about it, unless you've got a shotgun in one hand and a pint o' bitter in other. Other times they still go their own way but they don't know what way it is unless you give 'em a nudge. Hey! Let's get show on road.

*They exit together.*

### Scene Twenty Four

**PHIL** *is outside his house, back in his own clothes. He uses a paper knife to open a large envelope and take out a child's painting. He chuckles at it, still holding the knife.*

*He doesn't see* **JIM**, **HARRY** *and* **ANDY** *enter behind him, run anxiously towards him and then hesitate.*

**ANDY**  There he is.

**JIM**  Phil, you all right?

**PHIL**  Picture from me kid. Dressed as a clown.

**ANDY**  *(taking the knife from* **PHIL***)* Coming for a pint, then?

**PHIL**  *(looking at them for first time)* Drink with scabs, do you? I voted for money, you know that?

**JIM**  *(eventually)* Stop being a bloody drama queen, Phil. Come and have a wet with us.

**HARRY**  We were just on our way to see you and yer dad.

**PHIL**  Oh ay, I tell you if he were up and about we'd all be in intensive care.

**GLORIA** *enters.*

*Once again only* **ANDY** *will look at her.*

**GLORIA**  Can I talk to you?

**ANDY**  Ay, you can.

**GLORIA**  It's just for a minute. I wanted to show you summat. *(She produces a brand new cheque book and hands it to* **ANDY***)*

**ANDY** *gives the cheque book to* **HARRY** *who gives it to* **JIM**. **JIM** *turns away to study it.*

It's a new bank account in the name of Grimley Colliery Band. There's three grand in it. If nowt else it should get you to Albert Hall.

**HARRY** This your money then, is it, love?

**GLORIA** Some of it. I didn't get as much as you in the pay-off but maybe I didn't deserve it. Besides, I have every intention of working again. And some of it...well, you should know it's not just Danny's heart you'd break if you didn't go to London. Most of Grimley's expecting to see you play for them.

**HARRY** But everybody knows we've packed it in.

**RITA** Oh...we told 'em you'd changed your minds.

**ANDY** We?

**VERA** She has got some friends round here, you know.

**RITA** And, first rule of politics—

**GLORIA** —you need to organise.

*They're waiting for* **JIM**.

**JIM** It must be awful, love. Having that much guilt you've got to buy your way out of it.

**PHIL** Jim...

**GLORIA** I'm not doing this for me. And I'm certainly not doing it for you. Or any individual round here. If it's for anyone it's for Danny.

**JIM** But you'd want to play with us, yeah?

**GLORIA** Well...

**HARRY** Bloody hell, Jim...

*A pause. Like a good democrat,* **JIM** *realises the meeting is against him. Even* **VERA** *is glaring at him.*

**JIM** Budgeted for booze, have you? Danny would want us to win. Suppose we stand a better chance wi' a flaming flugel.

**VERA** Good lad! He is a good boy.

**PHIL** Andy! Your tenor horn!

**ANDY** *(suddenly jumping up)* Hell fire! Simmo!

*They all crowd round a table we can't see.* **JIM** *mimics the "whispering voice" commentary of Ted Lowe.*

**JIM** And it's all on the black. As Andy Barrow's twenty pound plays Simmo's tenor horn. Young Andy Barrow has this chance for the match–an oh so fine fine cut into the middle pocket.

*Click as* **ANDY** *strikes the ball.*

**ANDY** Oh fuck–I've missed it!

**JIM** *(still in a hushed voice)* Oh fuck–he's missed it!

**HARRY** But he's given it some welly.

**JIM** It's coming back off both cushions and—

**ALL** Y-E-S-S-S...

*As the roars die down,* **PHIL** *is left as the others exit.*

**PHIL** *writes a note to* **DANNY**, *puts it on the bed and tiptoes off.*

**DANNY** *wakes and reads it.*

**DANNY** "Dad, we're going!"–not without chuffing me, you're not!

*He gets out of bed and pulls his bandsman's jacket on over his pyjamas. Going over to the wings, he collects his bike from stage management.*

### Scene Twenty Five

*The Albert Hall.*

*In a backstage area* **VERA** *and* **RITA** *are doing womanly things to their menfolks' collars.* **JIM, HARRY, GLORIA** *and* **ANDY** *suck on last minute fags, wish each other luck.* **PHIL** *is solitary, edgy, determined.*

*There is a moment as* **SANDRA** *and the kids arrive, and* **VERA** *and* **RITA** *take them off to find seats.*

*As the band is left alone we hear a backstage call in a female London voice.*

**VOICEOVER** Grimley, you have one minute. One minute, Grimley Coll... Grimley Coll...er...ierie. Oh, chuff it, one minute, Grimley.

**HARRY** Bet she's glad they've closed the bugger.

*They leave to join the band.*

**HARRY** *takes up the conductor's position and, after a pause, they play the William Tell overture. At the end they listen intently until they hear the male Northern voice of the* **ANNOUNCER** *break into any applause.*

**ANNOUNCER** First prize–the new National Champions... Grimley Colliery Band.

*The band cheers.*

*An official brings the cup towards* **HARRY**.

**DANNY** *is on the stage before* **HARRY** *can take it, quietening the audience so he can speak. He places the trophy on the stage beside him. He remains a sick man, but is firm in his delivery.*

**DANNY** This band'll tell you that this trophy means more to me than owt else in entire world. But they'd be wrong. Truth is, I thought it mattered. I thought music mattered most. But does it bollocks. Pardon my French. Not compared to how people matter. Us winning this trophy means bugger all to most people–sorry–but us refusing it, like what we're doing now– then it becomes news.

*And photographers flash, TV cameras zoom in.*

See what I mean? Over last ten years, this government has systematically destroyed an entire industry, our industry. Communities. Homes. Lives. All in the name of progress and a few lousy bob. A fortnight ago our pit were closed. Another thousand men lost their jobs. And that's not all. Most of us lost will to win a while since. A few of us even lost will to fight. But when it comes to losing will to live... *(For a moment he can't carry on)* Point is, if this lot were bloody seals, or bloody whales or summat, you'd be up in bloody arms–but they're not. They're just men. Honest decent fallible men and women. And not one on 'em with an ounce of hope left. Oh ay, they can knock out a good tune, but what the fuck does that matter? Unless they matter. Unless we matter. *(He breaks off with an aside to the press)* Do us a favour and print some of it, eh? Just once.

*The band and the Grimley contingent in the audience applaud. The bandsmen step back and stay in loose formation.*

**JIM** All right, Gloria.

**GLORIA** Was that a thank you?

**ANDY** I've never seen him so gushing.

**GLORIA** Yorkshire men can't be caught showing their feelings, can they?

**ANDY** *shows his.* **HARRY** *steps forward to pick up the trophy.*

JIM  Harry? Danny said we were refusing it.

HARRY  Don't be soft.

> JIM *and* HARRY *are joined by their wives.* PHIL *is approached by* SANDRA *and* CRAIG *and* MELODY; SANDRA *runs a finger round his neck.*

PHIL  Does this mean you're coming back?

SANDRA  I dunno, Phil. I heard...

PHIL  I've got a chair now. No house. But I've got a chair.

SANDRA  It all sounds very tempting.

> DANNY *calls everyone to order by rapping his baton on a music stand.*

DANNY  Shane, lad.

SHANE  Grandad.

DANNY  Listen. Let's give 'em Land of Hope and Glory, eh?

JIM  Danny, that's the bloody Tory party anthem.

DANNY  Is it? Well, they can give it us back. Who's got land under us fingernails? We'll give 'em "enemy within". Let them hear this from Buck House to the Houses of Parliament. Ready—one, two, three, four.

> *The band plays the intro section to* **"LAND OF HOPE AND GLORY"**.

> DANNY *conducts for a few bars and then hands his baton and jacket to* SHANE; *the jacket is too big for him but he puts it on anyway and starts to conduct. After a few bars* DANNY *exits through the band with slow dignity. When the music reaches the end of the intro, the band holds a sustained chord under the following.*

SHANE  *(over the music)* Grandad? Does that mean everything's going to be all right now? *(To the audience)* I thought it would be all right. You do, when you're little. His lungs packed in.

*He calls upwards, to where his grandad might be.*

Catch me, Grandad! Grandad?

*The band attacks **"LAND OF HOPE AND GLORY"**, hard.*

*Blackout.*

*Curtain.*

# FURNITURE AND PROPERTY LIST

Please see the note on page vi regarding staging.

## ACT I

### Scene One

*On stage:* Pithead winding gear (set throughout)
Presentation baton, **Danny**'s bandsman's jacket (for **Shane**)

*Personal:* **Bandsmen**: pit with practical miners' lamps
**Vera**: bag of sweets

### Scene Two

*Offstage:* Union memo (**Jim**)

*Personal:* **Harry**: comb

### Scene Three

*On stage:* Baby in pram
Football (for **Shane**)

*Personal:* **Phil**: coins in pocket

### Scene Four

*Offstage:* Rug in bag (**Vera**)

### Scene Five

*Offstage:* Snooker cue in its case (**Andy**)
Euphonium in case (**Jim**)
Tuba in case (**Harry**)
Leaflets (**Rita**)
Bicycle (**Danny**)

### Scene Six

*On stage:* Table. *On it:* sandwich on a plate

*Offstage:* Trombone in two parts (**Phil**)

## Scene Seven

| | |
|---|---|
| *On stage:* | Chairs, music stands, instruments, tin (**Band members**) |
| | Football (for **Shane**) |
| *Offstage:* | Leaflets (**Harry**) |
| | Baton (**Danny**) |
| | Flugelhorn (**Gloria**) |
| *Personal:* | **Andy**: packet of cigarettes and lighter |
| | **Phil**: five pound note |
| | **Jim**: Two five pound notes |

## Scene Eight

| | |
|---|---|
| *On stage:* | Chair |
| | Table |
| *Offstage:* | Shopping (**Rita**) |
| | Shopping (**Vera**) |
| | Supermarket trolley full of shopping (**Shane**) |
| *Personal:* | **Vera**: till receipt, five pound note |
| | **Sandra**: purse containing little |

## Scene Nine

| | |
|---|---|
| *On stage:* | Desk. *On it:* phone |
| | Chair |
| *Personal:* | **Phil**: towel |
| | **Jim**: towel |
| | **Harry**: towl |
| | **Andy**: towel |

## Scene Ten

| | |
|---|---|
| *On stage:* | Shoes, shoe polish, brush (for **Danny**) |

## Scene Eleven

*No props required*

## Scene Twelve

| | |
|---|---|
| *Offstage:* | Euphonium (**Jim**)<br>Tuba (**Harry**) |

### Scene Thirteen

| | |
|---|---|
| *Offstage:* | Clipboard (**Danny**)<br>Gaffer-taped trombone (**Phil**)<br>Carnation (**Andy**) |
| *Personal:* | **Andy**: carnation |

### Scene Fourteen

| | |
|---|---|
| *Offstage:* | "Diggle" sign (**Stage Management**)<br>Four half-pint glasses of beer (**Jim**)<br>"Dobcross" sign (**Stage Management**)<br>"Delph" sign (**Stage Management**) |

### Scene Fifteen

| | |
|---|---|
| *Personal:* | **Danny**: handkerchief |

### Scene Sixteen

| | |
|---|---|
| *On stage* | Two bags of chips (for **Andy** and **Gloria**) |
| *Personal:* | **Andy**: packet of cigarettes and lighter |

## ACT II

### Scene One

| | |
|---|---|
| *Offstage:* | Euphonium (**Jim**)<br>Tuba (**Harry**) |
| *Personal:* | **Danny:** handkerchief |

### Scene Two

*No props required*

## Scene Three

*On stage:* Pack of cards (for **Phil**)
Balls for juggling

*Offstage:* Mug of coffee, lit cigarette, magazine (**Sandra**)

## Scene Four

*On stage:* Letter (for **Gloria**)

## Scene Five

*On stage:* Table. *On it:* big metal ballot box, pencils, ballot papers

## Scene Six

*No props required*

## Scene Seven

*On stage:* Trombone (for **Phil**)
Television set (for **Bailiffs**)

*Personal:* **Bailiff**: receipt book, pen
**Shane**: receipt

## Scene Eight

*Offstage:* Thermos (**Rita**)

## Scene Nine

*On stage:* Clipboard and pen (for **Danny**)

## Scene Ten

*On stage:* Clothes including Mr Chuckles outfit with receipt in trouser pocket (for **Sandra**)

## Scene Eleven

*On stage:* Soft toy
Few belongings, old suitcase, buggy

| | |
|---|---|
| *Offstage:* | Notice (**Rita**)<br>Large wreath (**Vera**) |

### Scene Twelve

| | |
|---|---|
| *On stage:* | The band's kitty tin<br>Flugelhorn and bag (for **Gloria**) |
| *Personal:* | **Harry**: money<br>**Andy**: money<br>**Gloria**: money |

### Scene Thirteen

*No props required*

### Scene Fourteen

*No props required*

### Scene Fifteen

| | |
|---|---|
| *Offstage:* | Euphonium (**Jim**)<br>Tuba (**Harry**)<br>Pit helmet with miner's lamp (**Andy**) |
| *Personal:* | **Jim**: pit helmet with miner's lamp<br>**Harry**: pit helmet with miner's lamp<br>**Andy**: pit helmet with miner's lamp |

### Scene Sixteen

| | |
|---|---|
| *On stage:* | Hospital bed<br>Apparatus for a drip and/or oxygen |
| *Offstage:* | Small wrapped box containing gold baton (**Jim**) |
| *Personal:* | **Band members**: pit helmets with miners' lamps<br>**Nurse Vera**: thermometer |

### Scene Seventeen

| | |
|---|---|
| *On stage:* | Job Centre board or newspaper |

### Scene Eighteen

*On stage:*  Hospital bed
Apparatus for a drip and/or oxygen
Bunch of grapes (for **Phil**)

*Personal:*  **Danny**: notes

### Scene Nineteen

*No props required*

### Scene Twenty

*On stage:*  Rope

### Scene Twenty One

*On stage:*  Hospital bed
Apparatus for a drip and/or oxygen
Reading matter (for **Danny**)
Clipboard and pen (for **Nurse**)

### Scene Twenty Two

*On stage:*  As previous scene

### Scene Twenty Three

*Offstage:*  Pot plant with label (**Rita**)
Bunch of tickets, list of addresses, tin box (**Gloria**)

### Scene Twenty Four

*On stage:*  Child's painting in large envelope (for **Phil**)
Table
Hospital bed
Apparatus for a drip and/or oxygen

*Offstage:*  Cheque book (**Gloria**)
Bicycle (**Stage Management**)

*Personal:*  **Phil**: pen, paper, paper-knife

## Scene Twenty Five

*On stage:* Award cup
TV cameras

*Offstage:* Cameras with practical flash (**Photographers**)

*Personal:* **Jim**: lighted cigarette
**Harry**: lighted cigarette
**Gloria**: lighted cigarette
**Andy**: lighted cigarette
**Danny**: baton

# LIGHTING PLOT

Practical fittings required: miners' lamps on pit helmets
Various interior and exterior settings

ACT I

*To open:* Darkness

| | | |
|---|---|---|
| Cue 1 | During introductory music<br>*Bring lighting upstage* | (Page 1) |
| Cue 2 | The band exit<br>*Bring up lighting downstage* | (Page 1) |
| Cue 3 | The men go<br>*Bring up lighting on house area* | (Page 2) |
| Cue 4 | **Gloria** goes<br>*Fade upstage lighting* | (Page 3) |
| Cue 5 | **Sandra**: "Shane!"<br>*Crossfade to locker room area* | (Page 3) |
| Cue 6 | **Women**: "Say yes to miners' jobs."<br>*Crossfade to house area* | (Page 7) |
| Cue 7 | **Shane**: "...summat to do wi' 'em."<br>*Crossfade to street area* | (Page 9) |
| Cue 8 | **Jim**: "Come on."<br>*Crossfade to house area* | (Page 15) |
| Cue 9 | **Sandra** and **Shane** exit indoors<br>*Crossfade to band room area* | (Page 18) |
| Cue 10 | **Gloria** goes in the opposite direction<br>*Crossfade to house area* | (Page 25) |
| Cue 11 | **Sandra**: "She never speaks."<br>*Bring up lighting on street area* | (Page 26) |
| Cue 12 | **Sandra**: "...want to be pitied."<br>*Crossfade to pithead shower area* | (Page 28) |

| | | |
|---|---|---|
| Cue 13 | **Rita** and **Women**: "...will never be defeated."<br>*Spot on* **Gloria** | (Page 30) |
| Cue 14 | **Harry**: "...any other way, Jim."<br>*Crossfade to* **Danny** | (Page 32) |
| Cue 15 | **Danny** "...we've got now, Arthur."<br>*Crossfade to house area* | (Page 33) |
| Cue 16 | **Phil**: "Oh, Shane, come on."<br>*Crossfade to* **Jim** *and* **Harry** | (Page 35) |
| Cue 17 | **Vera**: "Come on!"<br>*Crossfade to* **Danny** | (Page 37) |
| Cue 18 | **All**: "Yes!"<br>*Crossfade to general lighting* | (Page 39) |
| Cue 19 | The band passes a third time<br>*Bring up light on* **Jim** *and* **Harry** | (Page 41) |
| Cue 20 | **Announcer**: "And now the results from Delph..."<br>*Crossfade to band room area* | (Page 41) |
| Cue 21 | **Phil**: "It'll have to be second-hand"<br>*Crossfade to street area* | (Page 44) |
| Cue 22 | **Andy**: "Ay. All right."<br>*Blackout* | (Page 46) |

ACT II

*To open:* General lighting

| | | |
|---|---|---|
| Cue 23 | **Vera** and **Rita** run off in the right direction<br>*Crossfade to* **Andy** *and* **Gloria** | (Page 50) |
| Cue 24 | **Gloria** pulls **Andy** down<br>*Crossfade to house area* | (Page 52) |
| Cue 25 | **Shane**: "...for Armley jail."<br>*Crossfade to* **Gloria** | (Page 54) |

| | | |
|---|---|---|
| *Cue* 26 | **Gloria**: "But very tasty."<br>*Crossfade to ballot area* | (Page 55) |
| *Cue* 27 | **Harry**, **Jim**, **Andy** and **Phil** regroup<br>*Crossfade to group of men* | (Page 57) |
| *Cue* 28 | **Jim** and **Harry** exit<br>*Crossfade to* **Phil** *and house area* | (Page 60) |
| *Cue* 29 | **Sandra** and **Phil** go indoors<br>*Crossfade to light on* **Shane** | (Page 62) |
| *Cue* 30 | **Shane:** "Just when football results come in."<br>*Bring up general lighting* | (Page 63) |
| *Cue* 31 | **Danny:** "Can it?"<br>*Crossfade to house area* | (Page 64) |
| *Cue* 32 | **Sandra** and the **Children** leave<br>*Bring up general lighting* | (Page 66) |
| *Cue* 33 | Cheers from the band dying away quickly<br>*Start slow fade* | (Page 66) |
| *Cue* 34 | All rush to **Danny**<br>*Blackout; when ready bring up general lighting* | (Page 67) |
| *Cue* 35 | **Phil** sinks to the floor<br>*Crossfade to light on* **Gloria** | (Page 69) |
| *Cue* 36 | **Gloria**: "I'll clear my desk."<br>*Crossfade to lighting downstage and on house area* | (Page 70) |
| *Cue* 37 | **Andy**: "Are you fit?"<br>*Crossfade to dim lighting upstage with practicals on and lighting on hospital area* | (Page 71) |
| *Cue* 38 | **Phil**: "'Night, Dad."<br>*Crossfade to Job Centre area* | (Page 74) |

| | | |
|---|---|---|
| *Cue* 39 | The others trudge in the opposite direction<br>*Crossfade to hospital area* | (Page 76) |
| *Cue* 40 | **Phil** leaves<br>*Crossfade to general lighting downstage, gradually dimming throughout scene* | (Page 78) |
| *Cue* 41 | **Sandra** and **Shane** exit<br>*Very dim lighting with floodlight effect upstage on pithead winding gear* | (Page 80) |
| *Cue* 42 | Medley of sirens<br>*Brief spot on **Phil**; bring up lighting on hospital area* | (Page 81) |
| *Cue* 43 | The **Nurses** look at **Danny**<br>*Change to day effect on hospital area* | (Page 82) |
| *Cue* 44 | **Phil** and the **Nurse** leave<br>*Crossfade to **Rita** and **Gloria*** | (Page 83) |
| *Cue* 45 | **Rita** and **Gloria** exit together<br>*Bring up general lighting* | (Page 85) |
| *Cue* 46 | The band attacks **"LAND OF HOPE AND GLORY"** hard<br>*Blackout* | (Page 91) |

# EFFECTS PLOT

## ACT I

| | | |
|---|---|---|
| *Cue* 1 | The lights come up<br>*Sound of pit cage clanging shut* | (Page 1) |
| *Cue* 2 | To open Scene Three<br>*Sound of baby in pram crying* | (Page 8) |
| *Cue* 3 | **Phil**: "Come on, kids."<br>*Baby starts to cry; recede as* **Phil** *exits* | (Page 38) |
| *Cue* 4 | **Rita** and **Vera** prepare to watch the band<br>**Announcer** *on tape as script page 40* | (Page 40) |
| *Cue* 5 | **Jim**: "Cheers, Harry."<br>**Announcer** *on tape as script page 40* | (Page 40) |

## ACT II

| | | |
|---|---|---|
| *Cue* 6 | To open Scene Eleven<br>**Danny** *on tape as script page 66* | (Page 66) |
| *Cue* 7 | **Rita** leads **Vera** away<br>**Announcer** *on tape as script page 66* | (Page 66) |
| *Cue* 8 | All rush to **Danny**<br>*Optional sound of a siren* | (Page 67) |
| *Cue* 9 | **Phil** hangs himself<br>*Medley of sirens and men shouting* | (Page 81) |
| *Cue* 10 | **Jim**: "…fine cut into the middle pocket."<br>*Click as* **Andy** *strikes the ball* | (Page 88) |
| *Cue* 11 | **Vera** and **Rita** take **Sandra** and the kids to find seats<br>*Voiceover on tape as script page 89* | (Page 89) |
| *Cue* 12 | The band listen<br>*Applause and* **Announcer** *on tape as script page 89* | (Page 89) |

# ABOUT THE AUTHORS

## PAUL ALLEN

Paul Allen trained as a journalist in Sheffield where he still lives. In addition to *Brassed Off*, his plays for the Crucible Theatre include *Herod the Great*, *Jokers 1, 2* and *3* (with Rony Robinson) and *Breaking and Entering*. Other plays have been premiered in York, Derby, Birmingham and London Bubble, and on BBC Radio 3 and 4. As a critic he has worked for the *Guardian*, Front Row, Plays and Players, *New Statesman* and *Country Life*. He presented the BBC Radio 4 arts programme *Kaleidoscope* from 1981 to 1998 and then Radio 3's *Nightwaves*. He chaired the Arts Council drama panel and New Writing committee and has taught at the Universities of Sheffield and Warwick where he was Fellow in Creativity and Performance in 2006-7.

## MARK HERMAN

Mark Herman was born in Bridlington in Yorkshire in 1954. He studied at art college in Hull before first becoming involved in film while studying graphic design in Leeds, going on to the National Film School as an animator. The story goes that he was a contemporary of Wallace & Gromit creator Nick Park's and decided, rather than compete with such a talent, to give up animation completely and move into live action. The graduation film he then created, *See You at Wembley, Frankie Walsh*, won a Student Oscar. He followed this in 1987 with another short film, *Unusual Ground Floor Conversion*, and then, after a period of diversion writing lyrics for the popular 80s band The Christians, most notably 'Ideal World' and 'Hooverville', he made his feature length debut with the 1992 comedy *Blame It on the Bellboy*, starring Dudley Moore. Not a great critical success, Mark had to wait until 1996 for his first major success, which came in the shape of *Brassed Off*, which he both wrote and directed. Avoiding the pitfalls of sentimentalism, the piece was driven by realistic characterisation and smart dialogue and set in a non-cosmopolitan Britain, which Mark portrays in a sensitive but not overwhelming way. The beautifully shot landscape comes over as more than a backdrop for the action and, featuring a stunning cast including Ewan McGregor, Tara Fitzgerald,

Pete Postlethwaite and Stephen Tompkinson, the film was an outstanding success. Next for Mark was a film adaptation of Jim Cartwright's *The Rise and Fall of Little Voice* in 1998, not long after he had offered his sympathy to anyone faced with the challenge of adapting this very dynamic live show for the cinema. However, he rose to the challenge and managed to capture the spirit of the stage production while at the same time creating an original film. In 2000 Mark took Jonathan Tulloch's novel *The Season Ticket*, the story of two teenage boys trying to get enough money together to buy season tickets for Newcastle United and created the film *Purely Belter*. He then wrote and directed *Hope Springs*, starring Colin Firth before, most recently, writing and directing the very successful film adaptation of John Boyne's children's book about the Holocaust, *The Boy in the Striped Pyjamas*, with a cast including David Thewlis, Vera Farmiga and Sheila Hancock. Mark is currently adapting Brian Lavery's *The Headscarf Revolutionaries* for the BBC. It's the compelling story of four women's tenacious fight for more safety at sea for their loved ones after three Hull trawlers sank in as many weeks in 1968 with the loss of fifty-eight men, a campaign that became global news.

www.ingramcontent.com/pod-product-compliance
Ingram Content Group UK Ltd.
Pitfield, Milton Keynes, MK11 3LW, UK
UKHW021843210426
5322IPUK00022B/440